Joe

What a God Blessing . . .
knowing you all these years —
Hope you enjoy
Ron Ryder

Making Money Out Of Thin Air
My Life as a High Time Pilot

An Autobiography by Ron Ryan, Founder of
Ryan Aviation Corporation and Ryan International Airlines

Making Money Out of Thin Air: My Life as a High Time Pilot
By Ronald D. Ryan
Copyright © 2021 Ronald D. Ryan

Published in the United States by
Air Capital Press, LLC
Wichita, KS
www.aircapitalpress.com

First Edition

This work depicts actual events in the life of the author as recollection permits and/or can be verified by research. Occasionally, dialogue consistent with the nature of the person speaking has been supplemented. All persons within are actual individuals; there are no composite characters.

ISBN 978-1-7352519-4-3

Cover Design and Interior Design by Air Capital Press LLC.

Unless otherwise noted, all photos are provided by Ron Ryan and Ryan Aviation Corporation.

Dedication

To my sons, for all the times I was busy flying.

This book is for you.

Without the help and encouragement from my wife Renae this book would have never been written. Thanks, partner. Renae's father, Harvey Schmucker, also inspired me to tell my story. He was a cattle and wheat farmer, but most importantly, he was a great man of God.

Define Success

Joy in life is a journey,
not the destination.
I am often asked what I consider
success. My answer is not original;
I heard it a long, long time
ago. Success is the progressive
realization of the accomplishment
of any worthwhile goal.
In other words, it is the journey.
It's the progression. I tell my kids and
grandkids, "Live life like this was
your last day on earth, but plan life
like you are going to live forever."

Preface

Have you ever heard an older person say, "Man, how time flies!" or "It seems like it was yesterday that…" and shrugged it off, not paying attention to the words or caring enough to get the context? Once upon a time, I felt that way, too!

Now, at age 82, nothing's ever been closer to the truth!

In my case, life hasn't zoomed past just because of the calendar, but also because I've spent over 30,000 hours as a captain flying airplanes, mostly jets. An airplane is the best way for man to buy more time. You can get things done quicker if you don't spend so much time traveling, or you travel almost at the speed of sound. You can go half-way around the world in 20 hours, or all the way around the world in 37, which I have done, when we set an around-the-world speed record in 1988, traveling at an average speed of 685 miles per hour, almost the speed of sound in a Boeing 747SP.

Since beginning my flying career at age 23, I've flown over 30 kinds of aircraft. Most captains may average 10,000 flying hours in a career. Airline pilots are limited by 100 hours per month or 1,000 hours a year flying time, and very few pilots ever fly as many as 30,000 hours, thus the classification as "A High Time Pilot."

I consider myself to be a very normal person and have no extraordinary talents unless it is flying planes. My primary education has been the school of hard knocks and bumps.

I suppose my experiences, both good and not so hot, have exceeded those most people have throughout their lives. At first glance, they may seem incredible, even unbelievable, these opportunities I've been granted. As you'll note, more than a few of them could have cost me my life.

Over time, here and there, I've related some of those experiences to gathered listeners, with only slight and totally forgivable exaggeration. Comments have been, "Ron, you need to get this stuff written down!"

This then, my autobiography, is my effort to get some of my adventures in some semblance of formation. Although, there are some stories I am not willing to tell and hope no one ever finds out.

What follows is a collection of personal experiences and recollections from across my life. Where dates are important, I'll say so. Otherwise, the events and consequences deriving from them are the point. It is enough to know they happened, and that they happened and I'm still here.

I have been very fortunate and lucky throughout my life. I think what I am trying to say is, if I could do it, anyone who really tries should also be able to live a fulfilling life.

My life has gone by incredibly fast; it's like a good, big blur. When I start talking time now, I have to think, "How many years have I been married to Renae?" Answer 32. I always remember that, and that concept of time helps.

I feel blessed, lucky. If I drop dead tomorrow, I feel I know what side of eternity I will be on. When I meet my Maker, I'm thinking the first question He will ask is, "Ryan, you have no idea how many angels I used up on you, do you?"

Nope. But considering the other conversations He's had with me, I'm thinking He's going to tell me.

These are a few of the people I really want to thank for helping me have a good life. My wife and soulmate, Renae; my siblings, Wayne, Charlene, Marilyn, Larry and Bobby; Grandpa Ryan, Jack and Sandi McInteer, Derry and Kay Larson, George Ablah, Jeff Crippen, Ray Thomas, Beth Paladino, Jack DeBoer, Tim Bonnell, Harv and Carrie Schmucker, Bob Hoover, Clay Lacy, Gene and Joyce Williams. If I tried to name them all, it would take a separate book, but thank you all.

Daniel Boone, a retired Air Force officer, took the first crack at some much needed wordsmithing of my stories, followed up by a good friend, Joyce Williams, the widow of my great friend Gene Williams, who married Renae and me in 1989. Joyce has written a few books of her own and reviewed some parts of the book I had written early on. Finally, it was Jo Lena Johnson who has done the majority of the work putting this book together. Mandy, the daughter of good friends Ed and Mary Sykes, helped to take a text file and create an actual book with pictures and all. Paul Bowen, an amazing aviation photographer and also a wonderful friend, assisted with some of the photographs and design. Thank you all for helping me put my stories out to the public.

Table of Contents

My Friend, George Ablah

The Emery Air Freight Saga

The First Airline 1980-1986

In the Interim and the Second Airline

The Argentinean Adventure

The Second Airline 1988-2004

Renae and I

The Seemingly Impossible

Green Energy Ventures

The Business and Pleasure of Aviation

Reflections

The Early Years

*During my school years, I was
anxious to get out of school, yet,
time went by slowly. It was the
only time in my life that it did.
Summer to summer and Christmas
to Christmas seemed like a long
distance between times, and I
wanted school to be over and
graduate. It was the only time
of my life that seemed to go slow.
Now, it seems like yesterday.*

Burlington, Iowa

They tell me it was a typically cold, blustery day when I was born in January of 1939, just before World War II broke out. My mom, Mildred, was sick with pneumonia and almost died giving birth to me. I later told her I was a pain right from the beginning! Oddly, I don't recall if she agreed or not. I didn't press the issue.

Believe it or not, when she married my father Everett at the age of 16, she said she wanted to have seven kids. I have often said if I had seven kids, I would drown at least half of them, or myself. Just joking, I think.

We called Burlington, Iowa, home. It is a farming community of about 30,000 souls located on the banks of the mighty Mississippi River. There were seven of us kids of whom I was the third: I had an older brother Wayne, my sister Charlene, and then came our younger sisters Marilyn and Barbara, and brothers Larry and Bobby. All are still alive and well except Barbara who died many years ago from alcoholism. I sent her to rehab three times, but sadly I didn't know that each time her husband picked her up, he would have a bottle of booze for her. They had five kids. Had I been aware of what he was doing after she went through rehab; his life span might have been a lot shorter. Seems the only way he could control her was to keep her under the influence. I so remember my Mom at my sister's funeral crying and saying, "No parent should have one of their kids die before they do."

Childhood Adventures

We were normal kids, doing all those things society now warns are dangerous. Yet all of us grew up to be healthy adults. Our "large" two-bedroom one-bath home was located on a tall bluff where we often played. We would tell our friends "drop over some time." My sister Marilyn did just that. She was playing in a big box by the edge of the bluff and tipped over and went over the cliff. She escaped serious injury, and I think it was an angel's doing. How the nine of us survived as well as we did in that tiny house is a mystery.

We also played by the Mississippi riverbank. One project was making homemade rafts and floating on them down the river. My brother Larry almost got killed doing this by nearly being run over by a large tow boat pushing many barges.

In the winter we enjoyed walking on thin ice on the Mississippi River; hearing it crack and break would have given our parents a heart attack. We also played on and around the railroad tracks located just a long block from our home. The railroad had huge sand piles that were used for traction on the tracks. We would dig large holes in the sand and hide in them. One day a hole caved in on me. Luckily, my older brother, Wayne, was able to dig me out. Trying to explain to my mother how I lost my shoes wasn't easy as shoes were quite expensive for my parents to buy. None of us kids knew we were very poor, so we didn't act poor. One day my younger brother, Larry, was in the restroom at school, and another boy saw he was wearing my sister's silk panties. As the kids started to tease him, he told them our mother worked at J.C. Penney and this was the latest fashion. He got away with it. Larry went on to become a preacher.

Dad was a bus mechanic, while Mom worked at J.C. Penney as a sales associate. In the evenings, she also sold Stanley Home Products at private homes. They were called Stanley parties. I often drove her to these parties as I would do almost anything to get in more driving time. Mom had a green Pontiac with a straight-eight cylinder engine and it was fast. I doubt she ever knew how fast, but I did. Mother was a great salesperson. There was never a person she met she didn't like and vice versa, unless it was someone whom she thought was mistreating one of her kids or relatives. Then watch out!

My mother's parents were both farmers, while my father's dad was a CB&Q (Chicago Burlington and Quincy) Railroad engineer (a very prestigious job) and my Grandmother Ryan was a homemaker. They lived next door to us and had one of the first TVs in the city. To this day I hate boxing, as my grandad loved to watch it, which prevented me from seeing a lot of Howdy Doody and Mickey Mouse Club programs. Color TV at that time was just a rumored myth. Trying to get a decent picture required a lot of outside antenna adjustments. We had a grand total of three channels to watch. Wow!

Mom enrolled me into Cub Scouts, and I progressed up to Boy Scout, eventually earning the rank of Eagle Scout. At some point, my dad became a Boy Scout scoutmaster. Dad was so worried about me that he sacrificed his limited time to try to ensure I wouldn't go down the wrong path. It took me years to figure that out. I always thought it was because he enjoyed scouting and, looking back through the filters of age and experience, I am sure he did. But the real reason was, he was concerned about my wild nature and was trying to keep me out of trouble. For the most part, I think it worked. I respect my father for doing what he did. My parents were hard workers and provided everything we kids needed, and a lot more.

You know that old saying about hiring a teenager while

Ron Ryan, age 8

they still know it all? My dad had obviously heard it. What I'm trying to say is, I probably wasn't a model "Tenderfoot." Going on hiking and camping trips, sleeping on the ground and cooking out, I am sure was a real sacrifice on his part. One of my Boy Scout friends, who always called my bald-headed father Curly, went swimming at a sand pit outside of town and drowned one weekend. That was my first experience with the death of someone close. The older I get, the more frequently death steps in and takes a friend or two... and recently, I have been attending more funerals than weddings. I have some very close friends who have terminal cancer. I'm sure I will be attending even more funerals, unless I get hit by a donut truck first.

I'm getting ahead of myself.

Two adults and seven kids were living and interacting in a two-bedroom, one-bath home, and four of them were women! Oh, yeah – it had its challenges. However, I didn't know it was supposed to be easy; both Mom and Dad filled that little house, and us, with love, trust, and hope. We didn't know for a long time what 'poor' was; we always had plenty of good food to eat and we always had good clothes to wear - though the colors and brands may not have always matched - and we were well cared for.

When my older sister was 10, she became sick while at home. At the time, polio was a dreaded disease. Mother called Dr. Murray, our family doctor, who had lost a daughter to polio. The doctor drove to our home, diagnosed Charlene with polio and had her taken to the hospital. We were quarantined, and my brother Wayne had to have someone deliver his papers. I remember the substitute paperboy would not come close to our house, and he threw the paper from a long way away.

A brand-new drug (penicillin) was being tried, and my folks agreed to let them use it on Charlene. She was lucky, as she made a full recovery with no paralysis, but she didn't grow any taller. It was a good thing she was five foot when this happened. She was on the ground floor of the hospital, so we could talk to her through her window from the alley. She had tons of comic books and games. I couldn't wait for the day she would come home. "Where are the comic books and games?" I asked when she arrived home. I was told everything in the room had to be burned. I remember that day and my tears well.

At age 10, I began delivering newspapers and did that for four years. I had the largest route in Burlington which required two large paper-carrying, over-the-shoulder, bags. The age requirement for being a paper carrier was 12, but I lied about my age because I wanted money in my pocket. I like to think, although I started out lying, somewhere along the way I learned better. I "hired" my younger brothers to help me deliver my papers. There was a brand new Dairy Queen built at the end of my paper route. A 15 cent strawberry sundae would usually be their pay; plus that was my favorite.

Saturday was collection day; the weekly charge was just 25 cents, and that is when I learned some people would try to cheat a paperboy out of his money, while others would give gifts and purposely overpay or tip. I couldn't believe an adult would try to cheat a kid, but I found out in life there are honest people and some who would rather lie and cheat than tell the truth. This was an important lesson for me.

Mom also taught me a lesson about making bad decisions. One day while I was outside, she called for me to come in; thinking she wanted me to do some chores, I hid instead. She must have seen me as she gathered up the rest of the family to take them to Dairy Queen. When I found out, I pleaded and begged; however, she refused to allow me to go. I didn't appreciate this teachable moment at the time.

At age 14, I went to work at a downtown restaurant. I started out the same way anyone else does, by washing dishes. But I watched and learned, working my way through all the positions, including soda jerk. Eventually, I became the main cook.

That same year, I received a learner's permit to drive a car, after which I promptly bought a motorcycle. Driving a car required having another licensed driver with me in the car; not so with riding a motorcycle. Life was good!

One winter day, I was enjoying the freedom of riding my motorcycle to church, following my brother who was driving his car. I'd been puttering with my motorcycle engine and had the belt guard off. For some reason, I leaned over to check on the belt's operation when it caught my gloved left hand, pulling it into the engine.

I was on snow, and thankfully when the back wheel locked up, I slid abruptly, stopping me from losing my fingers. I finally stopped at a plowed driveway, where I could back my bike up and get my hand out of the engine pulley. Once I got back home and pulled my left glove off, we all saw my left index fingertip hanging there by a little flap of skin! Mom whisked me to the hospital, and they sewed the fingertip back on. It turns out, I'd cut a nerve, so it didn't hurt much, but it was pretty gross to look at. To this day, I can only grow that fingernail about halfway out, and then it falls off.

I have learned a lot of important lessons over the years, but this one is funny. A teenaged neighbor friend of mine told me his mother was still giving him his baths. I told him how silly I thought that was and that my Mom would never be able to do that to me. About that time, my Mom walked into the room and stupidly I said, "Isn't that right, you old bat?" Now keep in mind I had never been disrespectful to my mom, but I was showing off to a friend. My mother took a straw broom and started to hit me with it; it hurt but I started laughing and couldn't stop. The more I laughed, the harder she beat me. I ran upstairs with her on my heels swinging that broom relentlessly. I thought I could make it to my room and lock the door, but I wasn't fast enough.

Mother never said a word about the incident, but I would guess she and dad had a good laugh over the administration of justice. Not only did I learn a good lesson, but I think my friend still let his mother give him his bath.

Our family was very close to one another. My two younger sisters started dating early and created the only turmoil I ever witnessed in our family. Dad and Mom did not like the guys my two younger sisters had chosen to date. Although there were a lot of rough patches, my sis-ters Marilyn, Charlene and Barbara had some great kids and families. My older sister Charlene's boyfriend, David Crilley, later became her husband, and he was always a close friend to me. David died about two years ago. Larry, Wayne and Bobbie, my brothers, also have great families. We still love getting together whenever possible. We have taken a couple of cruises as well as a trip to Israel together.

We don't get to pick our parents or family, but I've been blessed with both.

The Ryan Family, from left to right Back - Marilyn, Charlene, Wayne, Ron, Barbara, Front - Larry, Everett, Mildred, Bobby

The School of Hard Knocks

Sometimes those little things can turn out to be big things in life. As soon as I turned 16, I bought a '50 Ford, 4-door sedan. I couldn't afford it, but I never let insignificant stuff like that slow me down. A $32 a month payment seemed like something I could handle, and did. Right after the purchase, I took my sister Charlene and her boyfriend David, who later became her husband, to Nashville, Tennessee, to visit the Grand Ole Opry. I also took a friend and his sister on the trip, and we had a really fun time. We started a highway race with another car and wound up getting my little old Ford up over 100 mph. Again, the Good Lord was watching over me.

> *Sometimes what you're choosing to do costs more in the short term, but that choice opens up new opportunities in the long term. On several occasions I had to take a step backward in order to have a better opportunity to move forward.*

As soon as we got home, I took another trip to Wisconsin Dells with that same friend and his sister. Once we got tired of driving, we pulled off the main road and found a place to park, so we could get some sleep overnight. When we woke up that morning, we were parked right next to a green on some golf course with lots of people around us. It didn't take very long for us to get out of there!

Starting to find out what it cost to operate my own car, I took a job at a downtown Phillips 66, the 24-hour service station. Now a thing of the past, "service" wasn't just a name. Employees did it all: cleaned all windows and exterior mirrors, checked all fluids as well as tire air pressure, pumped the gas as requested, did vehicle repair and even washed them. I figured if I worked there, I'd not only learn more about taking care of a car, but would have tools available and a mechanic besides my dad around.

I worked at the station nights - sometimes all night. I did this so I could justify missing at least one day of school each week. School and I didn't get along. After each skip, the principal always threatened to send me home if I missed classes again. Strangely, though, he never followed through. I kept my grades up, and he evidently saw something of worth in that young man. He kept giving me another chance. I always thought it strange, the threatened consequence of me missing school was to send me home. Go figure.

A Lesson on Staying the Course

Because Dad worked for the bus company, we could ride free, which I frequently did. I became friends with several of the drivers, and I'd like to think most of them enjoyed having me riding along, if only for company.

One day I heard sirens and ran several blocks to see why. One of my bus driver friends had just hit and killed a five-year-old boy. His mother had been across the street, and in his eagerness to run across to her, he darted right in front of the bus. Though the driver did all he could to stop and keep from running over the boy, it traumatized him, and he was ready to quit and go home. His supervisor, who'd also responded to the scene, told him what we all tell one another: "If you don't get back on now, you may never do it again."

Seeing and recognizing me, the driver asked if I would ride with him for a while. Of course I agreed, and after an hour or so had passed, they brought a relief driver and let my friend go and grieve. Because of the wise counsel of his boss, and his willingness to ask me for help getting over that horrible event, he went on driving a bus for as long as I can remember.

That, too, is a lesson I've carried with me. I can't tell you how many times I wanted to quit, but chose to stick it out and almost without fail, it was the right choice.

Colorado Springs

Billie Gahn, the owner of the restaurant, where I was working, had a daughter who lived in Colorado Springs, Colorado, who was about to have a baby. I can clearly remember that was 1956, as Billie had just bought a brand new 1956 Oldsmobile. She asked me if I would be willing to drive her new car to Colorado Springs, to take her to see her daughter. Would I?! This would have been the last week of my junior year in high school, and my standing with the principal was pretty low due to my absentee record. When I asked him, he flatly said "No!" When he found out who I would be driving (as they were good friends), he said I could go if I got written permission from each of my teachers. That was easy, as each teacher said taking a trip like that, I would learn a lot more than I would in the last week of school.

Manitou Springs and going up Pikes Peak were thrilling. When I first saw the mountains from a distance, I couldn't

Ron Ryan, age 16

believe my eyes. It turned out to be a fun trip, and my first exposure to a very pregnant woman who had a healthy baby while I was there. Plus, I got to drive a brand new Oldsmobile all the way to Colorado and miss school at the same time. Talk about a jackpot!

Minneapolis

That summer my girlfriend's dad enrolled her in airline training school, The Humboldt Institute, in Minneapolis, Minnesota. Both of us were devastated until he told us he had bought her a new Nash Rambler and I could go to Minneapolis with her and help watch over her. She took a live-in babysitting job while attending classes and I went to work at Garber's Standard Service at Freemont and Broadway, another full-service station. Shortly after I started there, the city began to expand the street right in front of the station, and I got laid off. That was my first experience with a job loss.

I quickly found a job at the Electrical Service Systems (ESS) manufacturing plant where they made battery chargers and other sheet metal products. I was operating several different types of presses, metal cutters and stamping machines. That was before OSHA. I discovered I was the only worker in the workforce of about 100 who still had all his fingers and, in some cases, hands.

One time while driving early in the morning to St. Louis Park, a suburb of Minneapolis, to see my girlfriend, I got a speeding ticket. At the court appearance, the judge revoked my license on the spot. I waited to talk to the judge and told him I was just visiting. He allowed me to get my license back as long as I went home. I still had two weeks before I was leaving, so my driving became very safe as I didn't ever want to see that judge again. I lived on the second floor of a bed and breakfast apartment with about six other adult men. The owners were very nice people, and the food was good.

My New Family and Career

My girlfriend completed the program and then we went back to Iowa; but she never used her airline or teletype skills to acquire a job. She graduated from high school a year before I did, so she took a job at a drug distribution center, McKesson and Robbins, and I went back to finish high school.

It was during my senior year in high school that something finally clicked, and I became interested in learning. My industrial arts teacher, Art Engle, was a man who saw worth in me. He took me under his wing, getting me interested in understanding and operating machinery. As a senior, I was not only a straight-A student; I only missed one day that entire school year! Art was responsible for getting me a job as a machine operator at Burlington based J.I. Case Company, which manufactured construction equipment. Talk about progress.

Burlington High School graduated me in 1957, along with almost 250 others. My jobs had kept me busy after school and on weekends, plus my girlfriend had lived twenty miles away. So, I experienced little social interaction with my classmates. When I turned in my cap and gown, that was pretty much that. During school, my job at the service station helped me justify (afford) driving so many miles. I have often felt I missed out on a lot of good high school friendships, as most of my classmates were really fun and friendly people. When I go back to

Diploma from Burlintgton High School

class reunions, I find they have gotten to look a lot older than I do. I guess they say the same thing about me.

I started my first full-time job the day I graduated, married my childhood girlfriend the following week, and a year later had my first son, Dale. I was making very good money at Case, but I saw guys a lot older than I was, who had worked there for years, making the same money I was, as a relatively new hire. More importantly, I saw a foreman purposefully set a man up for failure who was about to retire. He wound up fired and lost his retirement bonus and pension. I never knew why it happened, but that was my harsh introduction to the sordid world of trade unions versus corporate America.

On one occasion, while I was operating a lathe, a union rep came up and asked how many parts I had done. Taken aback, I said I didn't know. He forcefully advised me I could only produce so many; and if I exceeded this number, my "new" car might develop some driving issues. "You're makin' the rest of us look bad, kid. We got a good thing goin' here. Don't mess it up, see?"

I thought, Self, this is not the way I want to spend my life!

Then, six months later, Art Engle, helped me again in landing my first apprentice machinist position with Murray Iron Works building steam turbines for a dollar an hour. Since I'd been making five dollars an hour at Case, my boss told me I was nuts to give it up, but I made the change anyway. I can't overstate how important it was that, at this point in my life, Art Engle chose to ignore all my rough edges and invested his esteem and counsel in me. It's a lesson I've carried with me.

Sorting Things Out

One day while in Fort Madison, a town some 20 miles from Burlington, some friends and I drove by Sheaffer Pen Company's Tool and Die Shop. One of the friends stated that tool and die makers could write their own ticket. I remembered that comment and think that prompted me to eventually go that route.

Grand-Parental Reasoning

I used to bounce things off my Grandfather Ryan a lot. Since the railroad yards were only a block away from our home, I went down there often to bend his ear and pick his brain. On one of those visits I told him when I grew up, I wanted to sign on with the railroad. He stopped what he was doing, looked at me, and said, "No, you don't. You want to work for the airlines, because the railroad is abusing and taking advantage of its passengers. Mark my words; air travel will beat the railroads out of the passenger business, and all the railroads will haul is cargo."

I think Grandpa also invested in me that day, planting the seed that took root several years later, leading me into the field of aviation.

Sheaffer Pen Company

I'd worked at J.I. Case and Murray Iron Works for a combined total of two years when I was given the opportunity to enter a Tool and Die apprenticeship program for Sheaffer Pen Company in Fort Madison, Iowa, 25 miles away from Burlington.

Nothing was holding me, so I said, "Sure," and applied. They hired me, and I worked there for eighteen months until they discontinued that program. They then offered me a job at their parent manufacturing plant. Wanting to finish what I'd started, I instead began hunting for another Tool and Die apprenticeship program.

One was with the CB&Q Railroad Shops in West Burlington, and though they did offer me a job, it didn't feel right and wasn't a good fit.

I drove 117 miles to Peoria, Illinois, to interview with Caterpillar where I was once again offered a job. It did look more interesting, but still wasn't what I was wanting. My former boss with Sheaffer Pen's Tool and Die Shop called me, saying he'd heard one of the Bell Telephone system's companies, Western Electric, was starting a new factory in Lee's Summit, Missouri, just outside Kansas City.

Driving five and a half hours, I arrived in Lee's Summit to find a temporary pilot plant in Grandview, Missouri, while Western Electric was building a massive new plant in Lee's Summit. On the drive from Burlington, I got stopped late at night in Independence, Missouri, where the cop said I was speeding. There was a speed limit during the day and a different limit at night. The lower nighttime speed limit was in small letters on the sign. They had me and another car stopped for the same thing. They had us follow them to the police station and wanted to see how much money we had on us. I had hidden all but a few dollars in the car

Valued Sheaffer Pen

on the way over, so when they didn't see much money on either of us they said, "Just get out of here and slow down!" That was my introduction to the big city life.

Kansas City Here I Come

Western Electric's apprenticeship program normally took four years to complete. Me being me, and with over three years' of apprenticeship experience under my belt, I managed to convince the man who hired me to waive the absolute six-month minimum time-on-machine requirement, letting me progress on as soon as I proved to my supervisor I'd mastered the machine assigned to me. A pattern seemed to be emerging. I've never thought much of status-quo or cattle-herd thinking.

The hands-on machine portion normally took two years, with the following two years working on the bench making tools and dies. Due to my previous experience, I completed the entire four year program in two years, reaching my goal of graduating as a Certified Tool & Die Maker. And because some of the supervisors had observed and trusted my work, they allowed me to build some dies off-schedule.

Employee Photo for Western Electric

We were making thousands of transistors; yet the process was slow and unreliable. I pondered that process, then built a progressive die where we could draw and stamp out thousands of the cases for the transistor. That's in comparison to the hundred or so they'd previously been able to produce in an hour. I also built a die during that time that stamped out a large brass chassis that previously required five, sometimes six steps to complete. Even at that young age, I believed in initiative and "thinking outside the box."

That die, however, was controversial, as one of the engineers swore we'd break the press if we stamped that many holes and cuts at one time. Naturally, our first try had a lot of onlookers, but it was a success. This willingness to innovate, combined with my having completed the tool and die apprenticeship at such a fast pace, got the attention of Western Electric's management. They soon offered me a job as a mechanical engineer, with the provision I attend night school and get my engineering degree. I was underwhelmed with mixed emotions.

I loved my job but, you guessed it – I despised night school. I drove a Yellow Cab at night to keep body and soul together in addition to attending night classes. In addition to driving a cab at night, I also sold WearEver pots and pans. The fun part? I would bake pineapple upside down cake during my demonstrations. The smell alone helps with sales. I then found I could make more money selling Kirby vacuum cleaners. Although I did not spend much time on either sales adventure, it was a good learning experience, just as selling at a Western Auto store in Raytown, Missouri, on weekends proved to be. My nights and weekends were used up plus I had homework from the college. I gave it a good effort, but after making myself miserable picking up 21 college credit hours, I pulled the plug and drained that idea.

With the "Big City" Came Big Changes

I was married for over 5 years; but after we moved to Kansas City, neither one of us was prepared for the "big city" life. The dynamics of both our lives changed so much that we each decided to go our own way. But we remained friends throughout our lives, as we had a kid to raise. Unfortunately, some young people act more from

24

emotions than good sense. Although maybe that statement shouldn't be confined to young people.

Growing up, I spent a lot of time on the river with my Aunt Red and Uncle Fritz Timmerman. They taught all of us kids how to water ski and would take us up to a cabin they had built on an island a few miles up the river. So, at one point with the good money I was making as a teenager, I wound up buying a boat since I loved the water, boating and water skiing. I guess you could call me an adventure seeker!

While I was single, I offset some of my expenses by buying a nice home in a nice neighborhood in Kansas City, and renting out two of the bedrooms to co-workers at Western Electric. They paid all of the expenses, and I paid the mortgage. That was my first venture into real estate and it worked.

A roommate, Dave Arn, and I were trying to break a world water ski speed record. (I think it was 102 mph at that time.) We were both able to get up to the low 90 miles per hour on a single ski. At that speed, it was like flying without any controls. You could feel yourself falling but unable to do anything about it. We broke several skis during this time. We wore lifebelts versus life jackets. When we fell, as we often did while skiing side by side, the one who fell was to hold up his hand if he was okay.

On one of our attempts at about 90 mph, I heard a loud crack, and Dave went flying, tumbling over and over as his ski broke under the foot piece. After coming to the surface, Dave was trying to hold up his arms but couldn't. When we got back to him, we found he had hit the water face-first, knocking all the wind out of him. He had then flipped over and gone into the water feet first, driving the tightly tied ski belt up under his arms, so he couldn't breathe. The belt was so tight, we had to cut it off of him. Thankfully, he survived.

On some of my high speed falls when I stopped tumbling and was under the water, I would need to force myself to relax, then I would start rising to the surface as I had no sense of which way was up.

Back then, very few boats could go that fast, but this particular Spiko racing boat with a Pontiac engine had two carburetors and could produce 550 horsepower. It seemed like we would drive the boat for about an hour and work on it for ten hours. The Good Lord kept us from killing, or seriously hurting ourselves. Even today, many young people don't think any harm can come to them even when they are doing stupid and dangerous things. I suppose that is not limited to young people either.

Education Lays the Foundation and Opens Doors for Opportunity
I believe in college and I also am a strong
believer in vocational education.
To practice what I preach, we have offered scholarships both in and outside the company. When Renae and I married we made a commitment to God and to each other... we both had a drive to help kids further their education and how we did that was to establish a scholarship foundation and have funded over sixty college and vocational scholars because we know what it's like to not be able to afford college or higher education.

Learning to Fly

Starting my career meant many jobs, lots of classes and making sacrifices in the journey to finding my true passion. A solid foundation built on hard work supported my journey.

Into the Cockpit

My first flight had been in Burlington. A friend, Keith Davis, had been working toward his instrument rating, and needed an observer to watch outside the cockpit while he flew the plane "hooded," meaning he could only see the instrument panel before him. The airplane was a tiny Cessna 150, but it seemed huge and exotic to me at the time. I loved it and was forever hooked on flying but couldn't afford the cost of the lessons. Keith was a sales representative for Sinclair Oil, a position requiring lots of travel; and I think he also had piloting as a profession in mind.

While working at Western Electric, a department supervisor who was a pilot, decided to go to the Indy 500 in his rented Piper Tri-Pacer. He took his boy, another dad and his son. The weather was bad. They should not have been flying but decided to "scud run." Scud running means flying beneath marginal weather where visibility is limited. He hit the guy wires, one of several cables supporting a tall tower, killing all of them. Even sadder, the

Trophy for the First Solo Flight

wife refused to go to her husband's funeral as she was so angry that he killed her son and her friend's son.

One day while still working for Western Electric and living in Kansas City, I was riding my new Honda electric-start motorcycle past State Line Airpark. On a whim, I went in and met Ken Fairchild, who was operating the flight school there.

Ken was a former captain with Trans World Airlines (TWA), which was headquartered in Kansas City. He said the State Line Airpark Flying School had a Cessna sponsored introductory program, and I jumped at the chance.

My First Solo Flight

I was able to take my first solo flight after just 6 hours of dual time. Some wannabe pilots take over 30 hours before they solo, but I would guess the average time is about 15 hours.

On my first solo trip out into the practice area, I thought I would do the easiest maneuver, a "power on" stall. Well, instead of doing it right, I used the "power off" stall technique where I pulled the nose up rapidly versus slowly and found myself in a spin. Fortunately, my flight instructor had shown me how to enter a spin and recover from one. Teaching that maneuver has been stopped now. I think I about crapped my pants as it scared the dickens out of me. When I got back to the airport and talked to my flight instructor, I thought he would be seriously concerned, but all he did was laugh. Since that time, I have done some aerobatic flying and still love it, as long as I am doing it on purpose.

State Line Airpark

I was hooked. I agreed to jump through any hoops they required, and because of Fairchild's connection with TWA and my intense interest in flying, he introduced me to TWA's chief pilot, Herb Kampson.

Since, at that time, TWA was based right there in Kansas City, and was hiring low- and no-time pilots, Herb encouraged me to get my license. He said he'd then try to help me get hired by the airline. With that strategy in mind, I went back to Ken Fairchild and began my flying career at State Line Airpark.

It might have been my age, or my starry-eyed desire to fly. Whatever "it" was, even the name – State Line Airpark – sounded exotic. I mean, it had over two thousand feet of runway! Why, a guy could operate the Space Shuttle from that! Or the USS Enterprise! I was nothing if not excited and determined. The guy who owned the airport, Don Fisher, liked my Honda, and I agreed to trade it for enough flying time to get my commercial and instrument rating. He had a motorcycle, and I had my pilot's ratings. We were both happy.

Flight Instructor Tom Hunt with Ron Ryan

Trans World Airlines, Not

In six months, I had my private, commercial and instrument ratings. Being young and full of my future plans, and with Kampson's encouragement, I went to TWA and said, "Here I are, a pilot. When can I start?"

Herb Kampson had taken me to the director of pilot hiring, who was also a young new hire for TWA. When Herb left me alone in the director's office, the director stood up and loudly stated he didn't like the fact that the Chief Pilot brought me in; he said he'd make sure I didn't get hired.

What a kick in the butt and ego that was for me!

When I told Herb, he told me not to give up. Not long afterward, I got a telegram from TWA asking me to come in and take some written tests. I am sure Herb got this step going. When he found out I'd been asked to come in, he said I could help him by allowing him to give me copies of the test. If I still did not get hired, even though I got a great test score, he would know his relationship with the pilot hiring manager was in a flat spin.

You know where this is going, right?

I got the test, knew the answers, and did well, as expected. When everyone had tested, the hiring manager called me into his office and said they weren't going to hire me. He gave no explanation, saying he had told me earlier all I needed to know.

I learned an important hiring lesson that day: Someone may look and sound sharp in a uniform, and yet be the worst possible match because of their personality, character and job performance. Later, I never hesitated to hire promising young talent. Yet neither did I use that as my sole reason. Believe me, I remembered that arrogant young hiring manager. I rather doubt he's considering writing a book and he's sure not remembering me.

Long Distance to California

One of my first long distance flights was in a single engine V-tail Beech Bonanza to California. We needed to be in Oklahoma City to attend my brother Larry's wedding, and weather patterns looked like we'd be all right. Since my dad's folks had moved to Sacramento, I believed we could get him there to visit them and return in time for the wedding.

On the way back, we had an unusual easterly headwind, which made the timing wafer-thin. Did I forget to mention I was to be in the wedding?

While at cruising altitude over the mountains, the cabin door came open. That can't be good. Although the wind and airflow will only let it open a bit, the noise and vibration will get your attention.

Dad was in the co-pilot's seat. Having the door right next to him come open scared him so bad he tore the upholstery off

Everett Ryan getting ready to board the flight to California

the inside of the door trying to hold it shut! Talk about getting a grip . . .

When at least half of the country you're overflying stands on end, there's no convenient place to land. I told him, "I'm going to pull up into a stall; when I tell you, push the door open some more and slam it shut." He must've been motivated, because just as the airplane stalled and I hollered, "NOW!" He pushed the door open so hard it sucked his sunglasses off his face! He slammed it closed and locked it.

We kept going and trying to keep the grin off my face, I told him I'd buy him a new pair of sunglasses when we got home. We just barely made the wedding, but the plane and the passengers were just fine.

The adventure was worth it. The woman my brother married turned out to be fantastic and she still is a great Christian woman and wife after all these years. Thanks, Gayla, for marrying my brother Larry and not letting me scare you off when I got you on the swinging bridge and scared the dickens out of you. Have you forgiven me yet?

On the Country Road

While I was a flight instructor at State Line Airpark, I got a call telling me to go to a rural area in Missouri and fly back a Cessna 150. A student pilot had taken the plane and got lost but kept going until he ran

28

out of gas and landed on a country road. Another pilot flew me to the location, but when I got to the plane, the wings were bent back and the control surfaces were broken. I asked what happened, and they said the student landed safely, had a farmer take him to a gas station, bought five gallons of gas, put it into the plane and tried to takeoff from the same country road. On takeoff, he hit a power pole and fence. Needless to say, that plane had to be trucked back to KC.

You're not supposed to use regular gas in an airplane. However, a little amount like five gallons wouldn't hurt the plane. But it was pilot failure since he hit the pole while he was trying to take off. He should have stopped earlier to refuel. He had flown over several major cities.

He was a student pilot on a required cross-country trip. In order to get your license, you have to have so much instrument time, hours and cross-country time. It was a bonehead move on his part to fly all the way to Illinois from Kansas City and then land on a country road. Had he just admitted his problem, a competent pilot could have gotten the plane out of there without damage. Between him and the insurance company, they were responsible for paying the damages. He ended his flying career. Seeing what happened to that young pilot reinforced the lesson: You should know when you've gone too far.

Fond Memories of State Line Airpark

State Line Airpark also had a hump in the middle, so you couldn't see the hangar rooftops to the south, nor the electrical wires and the tree to the north. Worse yet, you couldn't tell if there was another plane at the end of the runway you were on. Sadly, much later on, the owner of the airport, Don Fisher, was killed in a plane crash.

The last known use of that little airport was in 1982. It has been closed a long time in favor of Grandview Air Force Base and, later, the new Kansas City International Airport. However, that little humpbacked airport will always have a place in my heart. Unknowingly, it was one of the best places I could ever have learned to fly.

On my first solo cross-country flight, I flew to Topeka, Kansas, where the runway was not only long but very, very wide. I felt I could have landed across the runway versus down it. I had a terrible time judging my landing, but it worked out, and I made it back to my skinny, humpbacked runway.

Skyway Aviation at Ft. Leonard Wood

I loved working at Western Electric and liked my job. But knowing I had to get my degree, I sent resumes to other airlines. I also took every opportunity to fly and was getting quite a few weekend jobs flying passengers to other locations, as well as on sight-seeing trips. One day at work I got a call from Skyway Aviation, located in Ft. Leonard Wood, Missouri, asking if I was looking for a full-time flying job.

I went down there for a weekend interview and wound up flying almost 25 hours in three days. I quit my Western Electric job and went to work full-time, at half the pay I'd been earning, to become chief pilot for Skyway Aviation, and their first full-time pilot, as the others were all contract pilots. That may sound impetuous. I had a dream to fly. And I heard somewhere that if your dream's big enough, the facts don't matter. My dream was plenty big. In some ways, it still is.

Ft. Leonard Wood is a US Army Basic Military Training center that also has a military airport located in the center of the post, Forney Army Airfield, which Skyway used. This required that I have a base pass in order to get to work. We flew military prisoners as well as military officers using two Lockheed 10s, seven Cherokee 6s, one Queen Air, and two Cessna 195s.

My average flying time exceeded 200 hours a month, and I was in pilot's heaven as my goal was to build hours in order to increase my chances of being hired by one of the major airlines. At that time, the FAA limited airline pilots to no more than 100 hours a month or 1,000 hours a year. As I later realized, there were good reasons for that. However, as a Part 135 operator I was able to fly more.

We, Skyway, would fly when Ozark and Frontier Airlines couldn't because of bad weather, so I was quickly amassing twice the flying time of any of their pilots; plus I could get lots of instrument time. It was great! In my later 20s, I was young and brash enough to not think too much about how dangerous that was, and how lucky and blessed I was not to get hurt or killed. I wasn't considering my passengers much, either. After all, the pilot is the first one to the scene of an accident.

One of my most vividly etched memories is how poorly the Waynesville, Missouri, community treated the troops stationed at Ft. Leonard Wood. It never made sense to me; it was clear the town owed its economy to the Army post and the business its personnel offered. Home to the 1st Engineer Brigade and the 14th Military Police Brigade, the fort offered both boot camp and technical schools, bringing plenty of hard cash through the town of Waynesville. None of that seemed to register at the time, however. In all the normal moving tasks, like finding a place to live and getting a phone and utilities hooked up, I had to verify I wasn't military. Even the movie theaters mistreated the troops.

I never understood the civilians' thinking. These young men who were serving their country weren't being paid much, and for many it was their first time away from home. It seemed everyone joined in, taking advantage of them – especially every Friday night when the city dads conveniently looked the other way while the prostitutes and 'managers' pulled their trailers up just outside the post gates. It can't have escaped Waynesville that its steady flow of green came from the Army post and the various military-civilian contracts associated with life around a military installation. Nevertheless, relations between the post and town remained rotten, and the soldiers all left telling unfavorable stories about Ft. Leonard Wood.

Audry Glore owned Skyway Aviation and was one of the original captains for Frontier Airlines. He developed and certified the seventh seat in the single engine Cherokee Six. We would fly seven people and their duffel bags with a full fuel tank. Talk about an accident looking for a place

to happen! Another angel, maybe several, were on full-time duty.

On one of these trips, my Cherokee Six was icing up so badly, the vents in the fuel system were iced over and the tip tanks made out of a plastic material were collapsing. It's just not good when that happens. Thank God, the engine pumps had enough suction to keep me flying until I was able to get out of the ice!

Another time as I was landing to drop off prisoners in Detroit, I lost all electrical power. Upon landing, I found an alternator belt had broken. There was no one willing or able to fix it there, so I had them charge the battery. I had dropped off all my passengers, so I was alone. I advised Air Traffic Control (ATC), that I was going VFR, (Visual Flight Rules), on top, as the tops of the clouds were quite low. I dead-reckoned back to Fort Leonard Wood after calling ahead via land line while still on the ground in Detroit and advised them I'd be coming in with no radio. It was a very long, nervous, three hour flight. I found the field, and they gave me a green light to land. Upon landing, I realized how stupid I was for trying that. God once again had His hand on me.

On one trip while landing at Palwalkee Airport in Chicago, I was second in line to land. I saw a large fireball and lots of smoke ahead of me. The plane I was following crashed into a large building roof about a mile ahead of me. The tower asked me to verify the crash which I was able to do.

One night, Jim Robertson, another pilot for Skyway, was captain and I was in the co-pilot's seat. We were flying a Lockheed 10 into Detroit with a full load of passengers on a snowy night. The landing seemed uneventful until Jim started braking. The plane turned sharply to the left, and we went off the runway into the frozen snow-covered grass. Jim applied power and we taxied through the grass, onto the adjacent taxiway. The tower didn't see what happened, so we just parked at the FBO and never said anything as the plane was not damaged, but Jim's ego was. I was glad there was no voice recorder, as some of Jim's remarks might have melted the tape.

While flying as chief pilot for Skyway, I received a letter from Eastern Airlines asking me to come down to Miami and interview for a flying job. My hopes shot up like a rocket, and in a week, I was in the chief pilot's office being interviewed. After finishing the interview and taking some basic skills tests, Eastern told me to attend a new class they'd worked into their schedule, beginning in two weeks.

One would think I'd have learned from the TWA experience, but I went back to Fort Leonard Wood and told my boss I was going to work for Eastern Airlines. He was wiser than I and was upset. But he could tell where my heart was and let me work the two weeks prior to my leaving.

I had my stuff all packed and ready to go to Miami but hadn't heard where to report, so I called and asked. The response? "You didn't take a Stanine test, and that is a requirement for pilot employment." They said they'd fly me down to Miami and administer this test over the Easter weekend.

I didn't know what a Stanine test was, so I researched and found there was no fail or pass; just that you answered the questions the same way their most successful pilots did. The majority of the questions were stupid and had nothing to do with flying, asking questions like, "What were the recipe ingredients for different pies?" And other such nonsense. There were about 20 other people taking the test when I did. When I got back to Missouri, I got a call stating I did not pass the test and didn't need to show up for class.

Devastated? Crushed!

It comes down to goal setting.
Where do you want to go?
Where do you want to be?
What do you want to accomplish?
Never give up.
There's no shame in failure, the shame is
if you don't get back up and try again.

Once again my spirit took a real hit. I was sure this was the career path I wanted; but it seemed there were people and events in place to keep that out of my reach. As it turns out, I wasn't too far off course.

I called the chief pilot, but he said it was out of his hands. Lovely. Suddenly I wasn't as impressed by "Chief Pilot" as I'd been when trying to get on with TWA. I called the other people I met, and each one had received the same call: "You failed the test. Don't bother coming to class."

After some digging, I found this class was someone's bright idea and had been worked in at the last minute. Then, either Eastern decided they couldn't or shouldn't go through with it, or the union wouldn't let them conduct this class, so it was canceled.

Remembering my own disgust at the unions' abilities to take good things and mess them up, my money was on the latter. I had first-hand experience with unions, as I was the treasurer for the union at Murray Iron Works with the International Association of Machinists, and a shop steward at Western Electric Communications Workers of America. The unions, in my opinion, helped build this great nation, but left unchecked can also deeply harm it.

I could not believe any company could or would treat people with such callous disregard. I soon learned most of the major carriers had so many applicants, their HR types were rude and dismissive to all of us.

I wasn't flying the happy skies right then.

Midwest Learjet

Back in those days we flew at 45,000 feet at 550 miles an hour. The skies at that altitude were empty except for other Learjets or the military.

My hopes dashed but not extinguished, I took a job as a flight instructor at Fairfax Airport in Kansas City, Kansas. As fate would have it, Ken Fairchild, from State Line Airpark, had taken the position as head flight instructor and was quick to hire me when I applied. We worked for Midwest Learjet, primarily teaching students using GI Bill benefits through the local junior colleges. We had about 20 Cessna 150s, a Cessna 310, a Lear 24, and use of a Beech 18 for charter work; plus a hangar and office space.

Midwest Learjet was also a dealer set up to sell Learjets, built in Wichita, Kansas, since Bill Lear had started selling his planes through dealerships much like the auto industry still does today. That Lear 24 had the serial number 125; it's the first one I learned to fly. I was grieved to hear this plane went down in Alaska some years ago with the loss of all on board.

An Almost Run-in with a President

While I was flight instructing at Fairfax Airport I lived in Independence, Missouri. While driving to work, a Plymouth pulled out right in front of me and I had to slam on my brakes to avoid hitting it. I honked my horn and waited as the person who drove out of a driveway right in front of me didn't stop but just drove on. When I started up again, I was immediately stopped by an unmarked police car. The man who came up to my car turned out to be a secret service agent. He asked me if I knew who I almost hit and I said no. He said "Well, that was Harry Truman and he is a terrible driver." He went on to say they wished

he didn't drive himself but that was his choice. He wished me a good day and told me to drive on.

Flying High with The Colonel

One of the most colorful, unlikely flight instructors I ever had was Earl Myers. He was the Lear Captain for Midwest Learjet and was also a retired bird colonel. Yeah, unfortunately, one of "those" guys who let his title go to his head. I must say almost all of the Air Force personnel, including Colonels and Generals, I have met have been the best of the best, and I have met a lot of them. I deeply respect what they do for our country.

Earl expected everyone to refer to him as "The Colonel." He was a good stick man – an accomplished and competent pilot – yet, he had his share of bad habits. With all that, every pilot in Midwest Learjet coveted being Myers' co-pilot. I was no exception. But as a mere charter pilot and young flight instructor, I knew I had as much chance being the Colonel's co-pilot as he did becoming the officer and gentleman he was trying so hard to portray.

On a bright, sunny day for which Kansas is known, one of Midwest Learjet Corporate's three owners asked me to fly him in the Cessna 310 to Omaha for a business trip. The flight there was uneventful; the return trip was anything but. Approaching Fairfax Airport, when I tried to lower the landing gear, I heard a hideous grinding noise.

As the guy flying the plane, that ain't something you want to hear; it wasn't supposed to do that.

The zippy little Cessna's gear had extended halfway and had frozen in place. With no lights indicating my gear down and locked, I tried to lower it using the emergency gear extension chain. I guess I was motivated, because I pulled so hard, I broke the chain that operated it!

That wasn't good, either. I couldn't lower and lock the gear, nor could I raise it back up, which would have been better than half up or down – landing with the gear half-extended was the worse condition you could have. There was nothing else to do, but to land the aircraft that way.

The owner/passenger was scared to death, and in the excitement of those moments, he promised me a million dollars if I got him down safely. Being from Kansas, I'd heard the wind blow before, plus I was a little busy making sure we both landed safely. I mean, I was on that plane, too. Remember, the pilot is the first one to arrive at the scene of the accident.

Letting the tower know what was happening, I declared an emergency and took several laps around the airport to burn off fuel and give emergency crews time to get in place. I also had my passenger crawl into the back, and then I popped the door loose so we could get out if the plane flipped over. They wanted to foam the runway, but I chose to land on the grass to cut down on the possibility of fire.

On final, I feathered and toggled the starboard engine, so the two-bladed prop was horizontal. Just as we flew over the levee surrounding the airport, I feathered the port engine. It stopped in the horizontal position, too. One of those angels I mentioned before was on OT. I touched down on the grass; we landed smoothly and slowly.

The offending gear collapsed up into the up-and-locked position once ground pressure was applied to its outside edge. There seemed to be no damage to either the gear or the plane!

My grateful passenger and I slid on the grass for what seemed like two football fields, but it was actually less than 200 feet. As soon as the plane stopped moving, we both jumped out and got away from the aircraft. There was some friction smoke, so the fire crews wanted to foam down the plane. After some spirited discussion and shameless begging on my part, I convinced them the foam would do more damage than the belly landing had.

Once we jacked the plane up, we saw that the bull gear worm screw had come loose, pierced the side of the cast iron casing, and locked everything up tight. Thankfully, because there was no damage to the 310, the FAA agreed to file an incident report instead of an accident report. For that, I was grateful; accident reports don't fly well on a pilot's resume. The incident did however make the front page of the KC newspaper.

My boss/passenger was also grateful, but forgetful. In all the excitement and joy, the promised million dollars morphed into a nice steak dinner. As it turns out, dessert

News article regarding belly landing

was even better. This personal adventure involving one of Midwest's owners locked in a whole new flying career for me.

You guessed it! The company sent me to Learjet school in Wichita and I became The Colonel's co-pilot.

Now, the Lear was, and still is, a great airplane. In 1965, it was one of the fastest flying and climbing general aviation airframes built. Its cruise speed was in excess of 550 miles per hour, and we could fly up to forty-five thousand feet, well above most weather. I loved flying that bird! Earl kind of came with that, which was a mixed blessing.

All our maintenance was done in Wichita's Lear factory, which usually required one or two days on the ground. Whenever we'd land, the Colonel immediately headed for the Diamond Inn, located near Wichita's Mid-Continent Airport. He favored Scotch, and I couldn't stand the Scotch or drinking that early in the day. Unfortunately, I got so many of his drinks by mistake that I eventually acquired a taste for Scotch, which remains with me to this day.

On takeoff, we were usually restricted by departure control to five thousand feet until cleared to climb higher. We didn't yet have height-reporting transponders, so Earl would rocket right through our assigned altitude, and then have me lie to the controllers about the altitude we were maintaining or passing through. From the cockpit, that might've been fun. At some point, I began thinking about what it was like from the controllers' point of view, and what kind of risks we were routinely taking. A near-miss by a near-vertical Lear busting through my altitude wouldn't have made me happy, either.

Hippies

Earl hated hippies and long hair. He was The Colonel, remember. One day I was out in the hangar doing important co-pilot work, polishing our aircraft. Two guys with really long hair approached me and asked if our Lear was a charter, and what our rates were.

Oh, boy . . . I hesitated to take them in Earl's office for fear he might assault them on general principle. But a job is a job, right? Once Earl saw them, he asked who they were.

"The Beach Boys," they said. They'd been having such a great time in Kansas City that the plane with all the rest of their group and entourage had already departed, and they needed to get back to California. Once Earl realized they could pay, suddenly he liked hippies and longhair. Go figure.

We did fly them to Los Angeles and they did pay cash. At the time, the going charter rate was one dollar per statute mile, so that was a nice, prompt payday.

That didn't always happen. Once, we were waiting on our passengers, a young couple asked us what we charged. When I told them one dollar per mile, they said, "Okay, we want five dollars' worth." That was the day we decided to implement a minimum charge. One learns. I could write a novel about the Colonel, but he's received enough free publicity here. Besides, some things are best left unwritten.

About Safety

Safety is paramount, especially in the aviation industry. You don't take shortcuts because you can get killed or seriously injured. The problem is, we are people who are inclined to take short cuts and when we do that, that's when we tend to get in trouble. So even if you're not a pilot or not in the aviation industry, safety should still be a top priority.

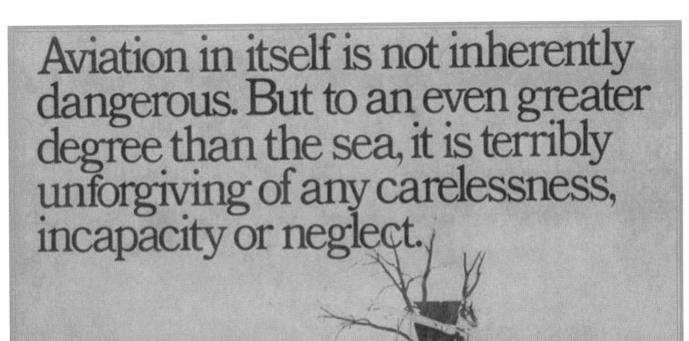

Aviation in itself is not inherently dangerous. But to an even greater degree than the sea, it is terribly unforgiving of any carelessness, incapacity or neglect.

The single most valuable asset any of us possess is our health, both physical and mental. Violating safety, puts those at risk.

And a few other things:

- *Being a hot shot can be expensive and dangerous.*
- *Know your limits.*
- *Be willing to sacrifice for your dreams.*
- *Pay attention to those around you, and how your actions, and theirs, impact all involved.*
- *Be resourceful, enterprising.*
- *Don't give up.*

From Pilot to President

The quality of my life has always been dictated by the goals I set and the journey in accomplishing them. It's not the goal, it's the journey. My journey was bumpy and swift.

DeBoer & Associates to DeBoer Aviation

I come from a family of seven kids who had nothing but love. That was great, but I wanted more. I became a tool and die maker because someone said those guys made a lot of money; so I set my goal and did it because ultimately, I wanted to make enough money to afford flying lessons.

I didn't know enough about goal-setting back then… being a pilot was a wish, even a strong desire. I had no clue that it would be part of my destiny.

DeBoer & Associates

A friend from Wichita called and said there was a new guy in town, Jack DeBoer, who'd been looking at Learjets and needed a pilot. An entrepreneur and hotel industry pioneer, Jack pioneered the all-suite hotel concept, inventing, developing and selling the Residence Inn concept to Marriott Hotels. Jack was himself a good pilot, but with a growing, developing business, he was smart enough to know he couldn't continue doing both and be safe.

I flew over to Wichita one Friday to interview with Jack. He asked me to take him and his building contractor, Jerry Gaddis, on a short hop in his Cessna 310. He liked what he saw and heard. The flight wasn't even over when he offered me the job and asked my salary requirements. I told him, he immediately agreed, and I just as immediately thought, Well, dagnabbit, I didn't ask for enough! I was excited anyway; this was the first time I started a new job making more than the previous one paid, and I would be flying a Cessna 310 versus a Lear.

I gave Midwest my official two-week notice and headed to Wichita, starting my new job flying Jack's C-310 on Thanksgiving weekend of 1968. I thought that appropriate, because I had plenty for which to be thankful!

I was the fifth full-time employee of Jack DeBoer & Associates. It quickly grew to a very large company, the second-largest developer of garden style apartments in the United States. Jack and Marilyn DeBoer treated me well, and I wound up being with them, and staying with them more often than not. Jack eventually made me one of the vice presidents of his company, in addition to being chief pilot. Jack's ambitions and work ethic were top-notch and he worked hard, which meant I was up early and late to bed most days. It was a good thing I was young.

The Virgin Islands

In 1969, Jack had ordered a new Lear 24B. He and Marilyn picked out both exterior and interior colors, and in my opinion, it was one of the most stunning Lear's ever built.

Getting financing for it was challenging. After flying different planes here and there seeking a lender, Lear itself finally arranged a loan through GE Financing. With that trifling detail out of the way, I hired Dave Lakin from Omaha as a co-captain, and we both attended Learjet School in Denver during the fall of 1969. United Airlines had a deal in which they would train all pilots on each new Learjet the company sold. The training was good. Yet, as with most ventures I recall involving major air carriers, the relationship between United and Learjet was a short one.

One of our first trips in the Lear was to St. Thomas, in the Virgin Islands. We had a full load of passengers including one of Jack's lawyers, Ferd Evans. Ferd was a bow tie kind of lawyer and a great guy. During our trip, we rented motorbikes to tour the island. One of his statements that always stuck with me on that trip was his comment of how he loved booze, bikes and broads. If you knew Ferd, you would know how out of place and surprising that comment was. When we got ready to depart, Jack was concerned. The runway was short, the weather was hot, and we each had a gallon of booze in our luggage. In the piston-driven aircraft with hot weather, this could be a problem, but not in a Lear. I jokingly told Jack we had about 900 gallons of jet fuel on board, and if he wanted me to, I could drain eight gallons from the tank to compensate for the booze. He then realized his new plane was a whole different world. The powerful Learjet airplane really is a time machine. It might be expensive to operate but used properly, it can pay huge dividends. Time itself is a priceless commodity.

St. Thomas Island later became a regular layover for Mike Sweet and me. Mike was another young single pilot I hired and trained to be a captain on the Lear. Litwin Industries in Wichita had designed and was building a large oil refinery in St. Croix, about 40 miles from St. Thomas, for Amerada Hess Refineries. We would fly down there at least once a month and stay for a week or so. We would drop our passengers off at St. Croix and deadhead over to St. Thomas where we would stay at the Frenchmen's Reef Hotel, later bought by Holiday Inn. We got to know the island well and loved those trips.

Aspen

Although Jack used the Lear frequently and wisely for his business, he also took some really fun trips. He built a large home in Aspen, Colorado, so flying in and out of Aspen also became a regular routine. I flew all the canyons and area on clear days, so I would know the terrain on the not so clear days. That experience paid off more than once.

Jack had a group of college friends who were all snow skiers. They called themselves The Ski Bums of America. I used to be an avid water skier and thought snow skiing would be easy. Boy, was I wrong! Water skiing and snow skiing are a lot different. My first skiing trip

Jack DeBoer and Ron Ryan

with Jack was to the top of Ruthies Run, which is a very steep, difficult run located right next to the town of Aspen. As he was leaving me alone at the top of the run, he skied away exclaiming that the last thing he needs is a one-legged pilot. I am sure he thought this was funny, but I didn't. I got

> *I did my share of hurrying in my early years. Why? Unknown.*
> *I was excited about life, about being able to make my own way, and most importantly; very lucky. Maybe it was a desire to cram as much living and flying into each day and night that I could?*
> *The saying is true:*
> *"The harder you work, the luckier you get."*

down the mountain after a long struggle; the only damage was where the tears in my eyes had froze to my face. I did eventually, and after a lot of falls, become fairly proficient at snow skiing.

Growing Pains

DeBoer & Associates soon grew to the point where I had to hire more pilots to handle the schedule. We also built our own hangar at Wichita's Mid-Continent Airport in 1969, since then renamed, Dwight D. Eisenhower National Airport. The hangar was more than large enough for our Lear, plus a Cessna 210 we'd bought, in addition to the two other Cessnas we still owned. With space to lease, we also took in the Coleman Company's Citation 500, Safelight Auto Glass's Lear 25B, as well as Cargill's Jet Commander. As we grew, I hired several more pilots. A few turned out to be bad choices, and others just had bad luck. But for the most part, our flight crews were first class, well trained, and safety conscious.

I hired a pilot by the name of Jim Sindo to fly the C-210. One frosty morning after overnighting in Peoria, Illinois, he used a broom handle to break the ice off the leading edge of the plane, resulting in leading edge wing dents.

The FBO notified me, as they didn't want to take the blame. When Jim returned, I looked at the plane and asked what had happened. Jim chose not to tell the truth, so I was forced to let him go. He went back to Kansas City and got a job as an air traffic controller and was doing well. He decided to have bypass surgery and on the second day of recovery, had some complications and died leaving a wife and two kids saddened by the turn of events. "There is no such thing as minor surgery," is what I was told while flying Dr. George and Dr. Jim Farha, two prominent surgeons from Wichita who are now both deceased.

Peoria

Jerry Gaddis, was one of Jack's top people in charge of construction. Part of his job was to fly to building sites for Jack and give a progress report each week. When he flew to Peoria, which is a union town, Jerry arrived at the site where he saw a bunch of workers huddled together, talking. Jerry demanded that they get back to work. The union leader walked up to Jerry and put a gun in his face and told him, the next time he saw him, he would shoot him. We visited Peoria a lot less often after the incident.

The Kidnapping

One day I, along with Bill Selby, a good friend and the owner of Fox Canyon Country Western Bar, attended a movie. Back then cell phones had not been invented, but pagers were. I got a page to call the local police immediately. I found out one of my pilots, Jim Oliver, had been kidnapped by some robbers who came to his residence. Jim told them he didn't have any money, but maybe some of his friends did. So, Jim was going to other homes asking for money. The police were concerned Jim might go to the hangar and fly the kidnappers somewhere. The police set up sharpshooters across from our hangar and we waited. After several hours, Jim was found in Kansas City. They had dropped him off. We found out later that it was only a couple of blocks from where they had captured the kidnappers. I told Jim with his big mouth, he was lucky they let him live, and I did understand why they just dropped him off in the middle of the street.

Suddenly, DeBoer Aviation

I flew for Jack DeBoer until 1973, when his company sank into financial trouble. At that point, Citibank, his main bank, advised him to liquidate his assets by allowing the various lenders to take back the aircraft and hangar.

Having Jack's lenders tell him to just let the planes be repossessed was shocking. However, knowing all the planes had equity in them; it occurred to me that we could start a jet charter service to at least help defray the cost of ownership, the goal being for them to pay for themselves. Citibank wouldn't hear of Jack DeBoer having any ownership interest in the new company, DeBoer Aviation, but they allowed me to sign a $96,000 note, more money than I personally believed existed, meaning I owned 20% interest, and his wife Marilyn owned 80%; but only I owed them the money. Not a good deal for me, but I felt good about this new start for Marilyn DeBoer. She was and is an incredible woman, wife to Jack,

and a great mother to their two adopted kids, Skyler and Penny.

My friends were nagging me, telling me Wichita neither could nor would support a jet charter service. I felt like I had to try, though. Jack owed Learjet alone somewhere north of $50,000 in maintenance bills; I had no clue how to pay them.

We had acquired a new Cessna 421 in 1969, and that same year built a hangar at the Wichita Airport, known by the three-letter code identifier ICT; every airport has a three or four letter code to identify it. The C-421, like the C-310, required an inspection every 100 flying hours, and we were flying each plane more than 100 hours per month. This meant more responsibility, and took time I sorely needed each month to get other things done.

DeBoer Aviation was growing, and travel demands, along with commercial flights, were more frequent. Out of necessity, DeBoer World Travel was born, and I was founder and president. That experience was educational, as we began working with all the airlines serving Wichita.

DeBoer Aviation Corporation Charter Service

41

In the beginning, we had ticket stock problems. The tickets were to be handled like gold as they could be used on any airline, at any time. We were required to have a safe where we stored these tickets, as ticket theft was a common problem for the airlines at that time. Soon enough, computerized ticketing resolved the issue.

I hired three talented women to run the agency: Lynda Tork, Jane Spurrier and Bobbie Hanson. Lynda managed the office, and the other two were travel agents for not only DeBoer, but handled the general public as well. The travel agency still exists today as Sunflower Travel, operated by Bobbie Hanson. Jane Spurrier also stayed on, and we still use their services for some of our personal travel needs. Devin Hanson, Bobbie's son and current president of Sunflower Travel, is a good friend.

The Lear Sale that Changed Everything

"Aviation in itself is not inherently dangerous, but to an even greater extent than the sea, it is terribly unforgiving of any carelessness, incapacity or neglect." This statement can also be applied to deal making.

Dee Hubbard was the head honcho at Safelite Auto Glass at the time. Safelite was doing well enough for Hubbard to promise Jack they would sell their Lear 25B to us as soon as they took delivery of a new Lear 35 scheduled to arrive in about a month. Super. Well, until drama ensued, as it often does.

Lears were popular, sales were booming, and the backlog for those tremendous aircraft was getting longer by the day. Demand and inevitable delays caused prices to skyrocket. When Dee Hubbard realized he could sell his 25B for more than the price on which he'd agreed to sell it to us, he promptly reneged on our agreement, selling it to another buyer for a higher price. No, we didn't like it, and yes, we'd have survived it. The sticky rudder was that based on the agreement between Safelite and (now the charter company) DeBoer Aviation, we'd sold our Lear in anticipation of getting theirs.

Underwhelmed and displeased works.

Jack and Dee were friends. Therefore, Jack asked me to sue Dee and leave him out of the proceedings. My mind did some muttering; it troubled me since I felt friends didn't knowingly do that to one another; yet I went with Jack to meet with his law firm. Attorney Wendy Snow listened to Jack's explanation and what he wanted. Jack introduced me, then left. Snow referred the case to a junior member of the firm who'd just hired on, Jack McInteer. That introduction proved to be extremely helpful over the years. He was, and still is, my lawyer and trusted friend.

When deposed, Hubbard protested he wasn't authorized to sign on behalf of Safelite, to which everyone had a good laugh. Upon the judge's order, Attorney McInteer asked Safelite to produce every document Hubbard had ever signed. Additionally, McInteer introduced into evidence the aircraft log books which had been meticulously kept by Safelite's pilot, Bob Wall.

They showed that Wall had included all passengers' names in his log. When Hubbard saw that, he ordered Wall to stop. To avoid further revelation, Bob then created a log with male passengers' names, along with the number of 'unknown females' on each flight. As it turns out, there were a lot of women being flown here and there with local businesspeople.

Wisely, Dee Hubbard agreed to a financial settlement versus going to court. I did remain friends with Dee, and his settlement helped us find another Lear.

John Rodgers, Just in Time

One of Lear's sale managers, Bob Woolen, called me the day after I'd signed the note with Citibank for the $96,000 and asked if I'd be willing to go to Dallas, Texas, with the Lear and be a pilot for John Rodgers, Texas Industries' largest stockholder. He'd bought a new Lear 25C and delivery was still several months away. The company promised, as part of the sale, they'd locate a temporary Lear for him. Having tried two other operators and declining their services, he was ready for a good one.

Rodgers had hired a retired Air Force-trained transport

pilot to fly his new Lear once it was built. Dave Lakin, my co-captain, and I agreed to train him in the Lear while on company trips for Rodgers. The Lear was too much for him. His decision-making was slower than the aircraft's speed so he was consistently behind the aircraft. He was a poor instrument pilot, which makes little sense when flying corporate jets.

Once while landing at Rockland, Maine, with Mr. Rodgers aboard, he came in hot. Trying to compensate, he extended the spoilers while still off the end of the runway. This resulted in a spirited and invigorating landing. The Lear was undamaged, but the pilot was encouraged to immediately test the possibilities for other employment.

Meanwhile, John Rodgers was wanting to add the new Lear 25C he had on order to US mega-conglomerate Ling-Temco-Vought's (LTV) Jet Fleet FAA 121 operating certificate. He asked if I'd do the same with ours to see how it would work out until his was delivered. As it turns out, LTV had leased several Falcon 20 jets and were stuck in that lease. Their growth had exploded, and they were also experiencing financial challenges. As a result, they had set up an airline charter operation to recoup some of their aircraft leasing costs. What's an operating certificate, you ask? If an airplane weighs more than 12,500 pounds and is operated for commercial purposes, it must follow the much more stringent FAA Part 121 rules, which are much more detailed and complicated than FAA Part 135 rules smaller charter planes flew under. I agreed to adapt the 121 rules with our Lear.

Our first flight with John Rodgers and family aboard was to their summer home in Rockland, Maine. The small airport in Rockland was located right next to the water without an instrument landing system. Quick-forming fog was frequent, often making it necessary for us to divert to our alternate airport, Bangor International. It was a busy place, serving as both a refueling stop upon entering and exiting the US and customs clearance.

On one such diversion, we saw a gaggle of emergency and fire equipment still scattered on the field. It surrounded a Lufthansa DC-8 which had experienced a blown tire on its takeoff, causing a fire. The fire melted magnesium in the wheels, which in turn burned right up through the wing. Fortunately, the aircraft was topped off with fuel, keeping temperatures low enough that the fire crews got there in time to extinguish the flames.

There were no serious injuries. When we got inside the terminal, however, we encountered eight very distraught female Lufthansa flight attendants. We happened to mention we had a large vehicle and were headed for Rockland. They asked if we'd take them somewhere for a drink, and we, being gentlemen and attentive pilots, took one for the team. Oddly, I don't seem to recall much more about that night.

John Rodgers was pleased with our services and requested we keep flying him until his new Lear was delivered. Mr. Rodgers' deal with Lear stipulated a set amount of money per month, but those numbers didn't work for us. Therefore, Lear subsidized the monthly payments by incrementally reducing, then eliminating our past maintenance bills. I've always been thankful for Lear's creativity. Had it not been for this three-way deal, our new jet charter venture, DeBoer Aviation, might have failed in its infancy.

After several trips, John Rodgers had me join him in the Dallas office. He offered me a position flying full-time, as well as managing some of his varied leased assets including several sailing vessels he kept at Rockland. I chose not

> *Money should never be your ultimate goal because you may wind up doing something you hate or becoming someone you hate.*

to take him up on it, as my loyalties were still with Jack DeBoer. Instead, I recommended my co-captain, Dave Lakin, for that position, which he accepted, effective when Rodgers' new Lear was delivered.

As such things happen, Rodgers' Lear was late in delivery, so we wound up flying for him for over six months – which not only paid off all our debt, but left us with some gas money!

Those months crawled by. Dave and I shared a motel room in Rockland while waiting, and it was an uneasy time. Downeast Airlines, based out of Rockland, where we were keeping the Lear while on any Rodgers' trip, was being investigated for violating FAA charter rules. The owner was threatening his flight crews' jobs if they didn't fly in unsafe conditions. An inevitable crash had occurred, turning a Twin Otter into a smoking mess and killing all on board. After four months of witnessing such at Rockland, Dave and I went back to Dallas where LTV Jet Fleet was based, flying from there for Mr. Rodgers, and handling charter flights for Jet Fleet.

The Omaha Lear Deal

We found a guy who had tendered an offer for Flavorland Industries out of Omaha who had a Lear 25B and a Cessna Citation he wanted to sell. Once the new owner of Flavorland acquired the company, he had the pilots fly him to see all the different sites he had bought. Upon the return to Omaha, he fired all of them and put the planes up for sale.

Jack McInteer and I traded time with the Coleman Company to use their Cessna 500. With it, we flew to Omaha to look at the Lear 25B and made a deal to buy it. Afterward, we had to fly to Chicago to get George Ablah's signature and meet with the Chicago Bank to obtain the financing. We got all of this done and flew back to home very late that night. I was flying the Citation, and Jack was in the back with the music up and a drink in his hand thinking about his future, considering practicing aviation law. That was my first closed deal with my soon to be good friend, Jack McInteer. That experience impressed me enough that

he not only continued to be retained by the airline, he still represents me personally, and remains one of my best friends.

Jack DeBoer sold the Residence Inn concept none too soon. He had worked his way back into financial woes, having a lot of assets but being short on cash. That sale solved the cash problem and then some. It couldn't have happened to a more deserving guy. Jack has also been a philanthropist, giving to quality causes both here and abroad, especially to those involving kids. Jack is nine years older than I am, and I continue to wish him good health. He has been a great asset to Wichita.

Flying Adventures

Life isn't boring, especially when flying celebrities, dignitaries and whales. Piloting around the world, providing excellent service, solving problems and making a great living? My reality began to exceed my dreams.

When John Rodgers' Lear was delivered, I flew ours back to Wichita, but kept our Lear on Jet Fleet's FAA 121 certificate. Whether prescient or digging into my flight bag of dumb luck once again, it was the right choice.

DeBoer Aviation somehow got the attention of Air Medic, an L.A. based company specializing in air ambulance trips for wealthy clients. They used independent charter operators like ours, taking a commission for setting up the trip.

Gerald and Betty Ford with Ron Ryan

Arrested in Nigeria

One such trip that sticks in my mind was to Kano, Nigeria, to pick up a Canadian citizen who'd been struck by a young motorcyclist several weeks prior. Because of poor medical conditions and resultant infections, death was imminent unless the patient was moved. A doctor flew with us, and the trip was quite an adventure. At one African desert strip where we were on the ground refueling, a sandstorm hit. We all got out and manually pulled the plane around, so it was tail to the wind.

Right-right. I know. Contraindicated. Yet, if the blasting sand had pitted the windscreen that would've been that. Since they had a fine gravel runway, which is a fine gravel waste left over from zinc and lead ore production, we arranged for a quick turnaround on the return trip, knowing every minute saved might mean the patient's survival.

Upon reaching Kano, we were told to report to the airport commander's office. They separated my co-captain, Mike Sweet. That's what they normally do when you're under arrest . . . And we were.

"Why are we under arrest?" we asked.

"You had no prior authorization to land here!" was their response. Huh?! Since it was a joint-use airport with both civilian and military aircraft cycling in and out, they were serious. I realized we needed someone with more juice than a couple of pilots could squeeze. I had them contact the United States Ambassador. I also got a quick call in to Kansas Senator Bob Dole's office; by that time we'd become friends, and I'd flown him around often. Between those calls, we made progress. Normally, I've no time for blowhards who waste time name-dropping and trying to sound impressive by who they know.

In this case? I was shameless in blowing as hard as I knew how! I made Kansas tornadoes look anemic. Nope, no apologies. We were a long way from home, on a mission of mercy, being grifted by experienced con artists. I was willing to use every key we had on the ring; I'd even make a few new ones if it would help. Hey. Juice is juice. If a little's good . . . And it was.

Senator Dole's office encouraged the ambassador to intercede. Understand, there was nothing racial going on, because I don't roll that way. Race, age, gender or education pale to me in comparison to what a man or woman is able to do. But in this case, it didn't hurt that the US Ambassador was black, as were all the other players. He quietly whispered for us to not try offering them money, which is exactly what they wanted, because then it would never stop. The line would keep forming . . .

From the airport commandant's second-story office window, we could see our plane and everything going on around it – including some staged drama by the Canadians. They'd brought the patient out to the plane and laid him outside on the tarmac. It can't have been lost on all involved how uncomfortable he was, lying out under the tropical sun, grit and dirt swirling around his pallet.

Letter from Senator Bob Dole

I try to never let a chance to exercise my smart mouth go by. In this case, though, I was as persistent as a Medicare insurance salesman who had my phone number.

I was able to convince the local commander that he was on his way to creating an international incident with both the United States and Canada. Showing marvelous command presence, he decided to let us and our patient board, and gave us permission to take off. Did I mention you don't need to tell me twice?

When we had prepped this little fuel stop, we told them we'd be on a short turnaround on our way back. Unknown to us and in a friendly gesture, they'd put fresh tar on their fine gravel runway. By the time we'd taxied in and stopped, we had at least six inches of wet tar coating our flaps and the underside of our wings.

With no time to dawdle and knowing we couldn't take off that way, we told them to fuel the plane while we all got jet-fuel-soaked rags and cleaned off the tar the old-fashioned way.

Hot, messy and slow? You bet. But it worked. Buttoning everything up, we taxied out and took off by staying on the extreme side of the taxiway, out of the fresh tar but just clear of the clearance and runway lights.

In those years, much of international over-water flight was by automatic direction finder (ADF) which used radio frequencies to help pilots maintain course. As long as the radio station was broadcasting, the signal would keep you headed in the right direction. However, you never knew your distance from it nor your ground speed.

We found ourselves off-course somewhere over the North Atlantic. All we could do was keep flying our base course until able to contact a Canadian center controller, who told us NORAD (North American Aerospace Defense Command) was tracking an unidentified aircraft in our general vicinity. Fortunately, we all exchanged information and realized they'd been tracking us. I was relieved to be back under positive radar control, and even more relieved that there weren't two Canadian interceptor crews suited up and panting . . . Those guys were some of the best in the business, and I didn't want them alongside my cockpit. Or on my six.

Canadian ATC directed us to an airport where we used the facilities, refueled, and continued with our mission. We dropped off our patient, and then headed back south to the U. S. When we finally landed in Wichita, we were all so exhausted we forgot to clear customs!

When I got home, I immediately called them. They knew us from our having flown so many international trips, so they said I could come in the next morning, which I did. More importantly, the Canadians called us a few days later. They said our patient would make a full recovery, but if we had not gotten him back as we did, he would have died. Another angel had interceded.

I have no clue what we were paid for that trip, but I'm here to tell you, it wasn't nearly enough.

Air Medic To The Rescue

Another memorable trip for Air Medic was on a Good Friday when there was a burn victim in Mexico needing transport to Los Angeles. Grabbing a respiratory therapist along with a doctor, we landed in Guadalajara, Mexico, about 6 AM their time. My co-captain, Mike Sweet, took the doctor and therapist in tow, and immediately went to the hospital to get the patient.

I stayed at the airport waiting, while the plane was being serviced and fueled. A short, burly Mexican man came out and struck up a conversation with me. He was friendly, saying he was a local sales rep for Cessna. He spoke excellent English, which was good because I spoke nary a word of Spanish.

As we talked, I noticed his eyes on the gold Learjet pin I wore on my lapel. I could tell he liked it, and he spoke of one day having one of his own. Whether speaking of the pin or a jet, I couldn't tell. On the spur of the moment, I removed mine and gave it to him. It was no big thing to me, yet I would be reminded later about how events tend to turn on the hinges of just such "little" details.

During our conversation, he asked why we were there. When I said we were an air ambulance and had come to pick up a burn victim, he became visibly agitated. As it turns out, a plane had crashed and burned the previous night, with one passenger dead, and another they suspected of having escaped the wreck and gotten away. My Mexican acquaintance continued saying the crashed plane had been loaded with drugs, and the authorities were actively hunting for the other passenger.

That was when an openly armed detective approached our Lear. Though he spoke only Spanish, it was clear I was under arrest and going nowhere. Mike Sweet chose right then to call and inform me that he and the medical team were also under arrest while still at the hospital, with no knowledge as to why.

I was doing a mental inventory, trying to figure out what to do, when my new Mexican compadre, proudly wearing his Learjet pin, pulled the detective aside. It appears they were friends, the Cessna rep convinced the suspicious detective we were an innocent Air Medic flight with no ties to nor knowledge of the patient or the flight he'd been on.

The cop left for a few minutes to verify what he'd heard. Next, Mike Sweet called again to tell me that though the patient was still being held, Mike and the medical team, including the patient's wife and a friend of his, had been released and were on their way to the airport. That was fine with me, since we'd already filed a flight plan to L.A.; I supposed that was where the party was headed, patient or no patient.

Two vehicles pulled to a dust-puffing stop in front of the terminal: the first held the doctor, the therapist RN, and Mike Sweet; and the second had in it the patient's wife and friend. The police paid no attention to the first vehicle, so Mike and the two medical types immediately disappeared inside our aircraft.

The second SUV was surrounded, however, and the patient's wife and friend were scooped up and immediately arrested. The Cessna rep told me they'd held off until seeing that the wife and friend were trying to get out of the country. There are some things I distinctly remember forgetting; this adventure was one of them. The more I found out, the less I wanted to know.

As we turned to board the plane, the Spanish-speaking detective said, "As long as you only take with you the same people you brought with you, you're cleared for immediate takeoff."

That was a strange clearance, since ATC was the only ones with that authority. Scanning the group, it sure looked to me like the detectives and their guns were pretty authoritative. We kindly accepted their offer and got out of there.

The minute we were at ten thousand feet, we informed ATC we were experiencing radio problems and would fly VFR to Brownsville, Texas. Asking a passing airliner on our frequency to also relay that info to air traffic control, we immediately climbed to forty-five thousand feet. Two hundred miles from Brownsville, we reported into their airspace at fourteen thousand five hundred feet, requesting flight level 450. We received an IFR clearance to forty-five thousand feet, so in two minutes, I calmly reported level at flight level 450.

ATC's "Roger" was accompanied by background laughter. Contrary to some popular beliefs, the controllers knew what was going on. We had already been there. We cleared customs in route and headed for Wichita.

Thankfully, I didn't have any aircraft problems because at that altitude it's about 70 degrees below zero. If you lose your pressurization, you only have 10 seconds to put your mask on (time of useful consciousness) before blacking out. Always be prepared to respond quickly and accurately. Fortunately, I have never had a rapid decompression incident but have several times encountered pressurization problems.

Elizabeth Dole with Ron Ryan

On the way, ATC advised us to call Air Medic as soon as we landed. Figuring we were about to catch it for the fiasco we'd narrowly escaped, we were surprised to instead be asked to go to Kansas City to pick up Ann Margaret. She needed to get to Chicago, so she could accept a Woman of The Year award.

Flying the Stars

After refueling in Wichita, we flew to Kansas City where Ann Margaret was waiting. Our Lear had a heart painted on the inside of the tip tank, since George Ablah, my partner, had that as his business logo. When Ms. Margaret saw the heart, she leaned over to show me the diamond heart necklace she was wearing. I'm unsure of the exact details of the necklace, but I did, ah, see more than that. Fortunately, both she and her husband were very warm, friendly and understanding people.

We flew a lot of celebrities over the years. I picked up Desi Arnaz and his son in Mexico and flew them to L.A. while Dezi was recovering from acute alcoholism. Fortunately, he made a complete recovery and later became a Christian. I had a similar experience flying B.J. Thomas, only his addiction was drugs. I also flew Lucille Ball and her mother into Aspen once. Monty Hall, Red Buttons, Bob and Elizabeth Dole, Joe Lewis, Neil Armstrong, Arnold Palmer, Geraldine Ferraro, Bill Cosby and many other "rich and famous" people have been my passengers over the years. Money and fame might be nice for some, but it has also destroyed many. Unless God is in your heart, you will never find real contentment. Having said that, I have been rich and I have been poor. I like rich better.

I picked up Bob Hope in Indiana and flew him to Wichita for a charity event. The tail number on the plane ended in DH; his wife's name was Delores and I told him I had brought it just for her. He laughed. He asked me a whole bunch of questions about Wichita and the surrounding area, and then used part of that in his show. What an incredibly fine gentleman. We remained friends after that.

Back on October 2, 1970, the Wichita State University football team was involved in a major aircraft crash in Colorado that killed almost all team members. Organizers created a fundraising event called "Night of the Stars," in support. We flew celebrities from all over the country to perform to raise money for the families of those who perished. Providing transportation to them was rewarding for us, especially under the circumstances. Quite a lot of money was raised that night. It goes to show what can happen when people pull together.

Kansas Governor John Carlin

One day I got a call asking if I would fly to Washington D.C. to pick up Governor John Carlin, whom I had known personally for years. He had been in a cab wreck going to the airport and had either seriously hurt or broken his neck and back. He was unable to fly commercially. I took the Lear, with a stretcher. Upon arrival, they had the FAA hangar open and ready, so after fueling, they towed me into the hangar and loaded up the Governor. I flew him back to Topeka, where he fully recovered. The governor's other option for getting back to Kansas was by ambulance. It made me feel good that we could be helpful.

The Achilles Tendon

On another trip in a Cessna Citation, I was flying the lieutenant governor, Tom Docking and his wife, Jill. While in Topeka, she reached into the plane to help herself on board but tripped the door latch. It tried to close and caught her heel causing it to bleed. There was a highway patrolman accompanying her, but he didn't know what to do.

To avoid scratching our plastic windows, we used sanitized cloth diapers to clean them, so I took a clean one and packed it with ice and put on her heel. We flew to Wichita and the next day the headlines were "Jill Docking cut her Achilles tendon in a plane accident." She was a good sport about the accident and nothing came of it, no law suits. When some people get hurt, they get mad at the circumstances. Fortunately, she healed quickly and we remained friends.

Geraldine Ferraro

One of our more unique flights was when we were flying Geraldine Ferraro when she was running for Vice President. She had chartered one of our Boeing 727s for a month, and for some of her flights, we had an all-female flight crew: the pilot, co-pilot, flight engineer and flight attendants. Although she didn't win the election, we were able to fly her where she needed to be, safely and on time.

During our tenure with the airline industry, we had a hard time finding women who had been properly trained to fly large aircraft. When we did find them, we hired them.

There were two main reasons for this shortage: the government was trying to get all businesses to employ minorities and women were grouped into that classification; It was also difficult finding minority pilots, mostly because they hadn't been trained during or after WWII. During their service they could not take jobs from men, plus they weren't granted military status until the 1970s.

No-Flap Landing

Another memorable charter trip was when Jack DeBoer and a group of his friends were going to Washington, D.C. (DCA) to visit President Richard Nixon. We were flying into Washington National Airport in the Lear 24B. On board were Jordan Haines, president of Fourth National

Bank; Dwayne Wallace, the president of Cessna Aircraft Company; Russ Meyer, VP of Cessna; Wichita's Mayor Don Enoch; Dick Upton, head of the Wichita Area Chamber of Commerce, and Jack DeBoer.

The trip was routine. Dwayne Wallace had a noise measuring device and was taking readings from all over our plane, since he was helping develop the Cessna Citation.

Returning, we weren't very far out of DCA and a long way from Wichita when I noticed the hydraulic pressure had begun to drop. On a Lear, the flaps, gear, and brakes are all hydraulically operated. The trip from Washington National to Wichita was right at the Lear 20's maximum range, so I knew if there was enough fuel to reach Wichita, we'd be landing way light. Conferring with my co-pilot, we decided alarming the passengers wasn't a good idea, and wherever we landed, we would probably be there quite a while.

On final approach into Wichita, I had to utilize the emergency air bottle to blow the gear down and make a no-flap landing. This is because although the Lear has an emergency reservoir of hydraulic fluid, I figured we'd be coming in hot and would need the brakes more than we'd need flaps. Upon touchdown, I activated the emergency pump and found there was enough brake pressure to stop us, even with the higher landing speeds due to not using flaps. Coolly, I taxied to the hangar as if nothing had happened. Upon deplaning, Dwayne Wallace got me off to the side and privately assured me I'd done a wonderful job. It seems he'd been aware of what was happening the whole time.

Emergency Landing Brings Bob Dole and Dan Glickman to McConnell AFB

Another of several eventful landings in Wichita was when again, I'd lost all hydraulic power and elected to land at McConnell AFB because Wichita's Mid-Continent Airport hadn't yet expanded their runway to ten thousand feet. I chose that because I figured I might need all of the twelve thousand foot long runway at McConnell. Because of my Chamber of Commerce involvement at McConnell,

I knew the base commander fairly well, and was able to pull it off.

Here again, seemingly unconnected things have ongoing results.

I used to fly Bob Dole around quite a bit, as well as Dan Glickman, and Congresswoman Nancy Kassebaum. At the time, I served on the Chamber of Commerce's Friends of McConnell board and was shocked to realize neither of those two men, nor had Nancy ever visited the McConnell AFB. Since I was frequently asked to fly them at different times and had always agreed, I sought the base commander's permission to land my general aviation aircraft at the base, so they could meet one another. I had the correct insurance and proper landing authority – but it helped to know someone. One doesn't just set down unannounced on a U. S. Air Force Base; not twice.

With both Glickman and Dole on separate flights, I had no issues landing on base. This, I'm convinced, had something to do with widening Rock Road and making necessary updates to the McConnell front gate guard shack to make traffic flow and control more efficient. What was to be a short meeting, turned out in both cases, to be rather long, more than one-hour meetings. Today, one of the major meeting centers at McConnell is named the Dole Center.

The F-4 Phantom at McConnell AFB

When my friend Rowland Smith was the Air National Guard Commander, he asked if I would like to take a flight in an F-4 Phantom Jet out of McConnell AFB. Obviously, I told him yes, so he set it up.

I had to go through the flight simulator primarily to learn how to eject should that be necessary; egress training is mandatory, no matter who you are. The night before the flight, a bunch of the airmen took me out and tried to get me drunk. I could tell they wanted to get me sick during the flight, so they could tease me later.

Early the next morning I got in the plane – or I should say they strapped me in – and we took off. Colonel Johnson was the pilot in command, and he immediately started putting me through a bunch of G-force maneuvers. We did low-level intercept flights and high-level air refueling flights. We flew in formation, even in the clouds.

The saying is true of the F-4; if you can put enough power on a brick, you can fly it. When we pulled back on the throttles, it was like putting on the brakes. We went up to the bombing range by Salina, Kansas, and did six bombing runs. This is where you pull at least six G's, which means six times your weight. To keep from blacking out, you wear a pressure suit that inflates to keep your blood from pooling while you are pulling high G forces. I never got close to being sick. I returned from that experience thrilled and happy.

Timing in life has a lot to do with life.

I would've been thrilled to fly those planes on a regular basis. I would jokingly tell my military friends I didn't have to serve because of my allergies… I was allergic to bullets. Seriously though, I was interested and wanted to serve my country, however, the Army would not take anyone

Certificate for K.A.N.G. F-4 Phantom Flight

with a dependent when I had decided to join. Since I had graduated high school and got married, in the same week, the Army would not take me. As a matter of fact, my recruiter suggested that I get a divorce, sign up and then get remarried. I chose not to do that. So, my timing was such that I wasn't required to go into the military.

From that point on, my timing and life was such that they never really wanted me. My life would have been a lot different. If I was going to go into the Air Force, I might have been happy but, probably not the Army, with whom I was originally going to enlist.

One of my friends from Kansas City flew a Lear for the Coca Cola bottler owner. They, like us, chartered their aircraft. We'd agreed to help each other out when the situation demanded it.

Denny, their captain, called one day, asking if I could take some of their clients to Las Vegas along with his plane, since both aircraft would be full. We got to Las Vegas, and in the time-honored tradition, scouted around to see what mischief we could scare up for four pilots.

Sherrie's Ranch was a brothel, located about sixty miles outside of town. Of course, one of the pilots knew the owner, and knew he operated a dirt/sand runway long enough to handle our Lear. The owner, always alert for publicity, said he'd never had a jet up there. And if we wanted to come up, everything would be on the house.

After lengthy deliberation of about three seconds, we saddled up and flew there. Thinking back, it's odd the air traffic controllers all knew its exact location . . .

We circled once, checking out the runway. Deciding it was okay, we landed with no problem. As it turns out, the Ranch owner was a World War II pilot and met us at the airplane. Two of us four pilots had agreed beforehand not to drink, so we could fly ourselves home. I was one of the two, not realizing we would be spending most of the afternoon there. Seeing a Learjet parked outside Sherrie's Ranch was something new and folks were stopping to see the jet. Right.

For months afterward, we figured the euphemism for

visiting the Ranch was, "We just went out there to see the jet." When we finally did take off, our Lear was full because several visitors to the Ranch wanted to ride back to Vegas with us, and then decide how to get home from there.

Ranch sounds impressive. The place was actually little more than a few trailer houses parked close enough together to share lights and utilities from a common pole. When we taxied out and onto the runway on the end opposite the trailers and power pole, we could feel the aircraft sinking into the sand. Throttling up in a Lear is an impressive feeling; even fully loaded, we were quickly airborne.

I'm not sure what came over me, but I held the nose down, quickly accelerating as I retracted our gear. We shot right over those trailers at the opposite end of the runway! We were chuckling, but as we looked back, we saw a huge rooster tail of dust settling back down in our wake.

Though I hate to admit it, pilots aren't always the brightest. It seems one of the guys had fallen deeply in like with one of the Ranch girls and tried to call her once we'd landed back in Las Vegas. He couldn't get through because, strangely, the phones weren't working. The results of our ultra-low, high-speed pass over those trailers took out the phone and power lines. Oops! We thought it best we keep our heads down, mouths shut, and after a couple of days' down time, headed back to Kansas City and Wichita.

Non-Traditional Passengers

One might be surprised how much the military and government use commercial airlines and charter operators to transport all kinds of things and people. Over the years, between our human passengers and live cargo, we had some adventures. We have carried gorillas, fish, mice, monkeys and a lot of squirrely folks over the years. We flew horses, primarily out of Louisville, Kentucky, and one of our more interesting passengers was Shamu the whale, who we flew from Miami to San Diego. Talk about a big bathtub!

One day we were asked to fly to Chicago's O'Hare International Airport by the National Basketball Association, with one of the five sports/entertainer B-727s we were operating. They had us park next to a competitor of ours, Sport Hawk. Soon enough, a long limo drove up and this very tall guy got out. He walked through both planes and then left. We found out Michael Jordan was looking for a plane to travel in while he was a member of the Dream Team. He selected our plane.

Later we asked, "Why ours?" We were told he was being paid the maximum on the salary cap and any perks they could give him helped. Picking the plane he wanted to fly in was one of his perks.

We flew the Chicago Bulls as well as some other basketball teams for a couple of seasons and loved it, although at times, flying professional athletes presented its challenges. Most players were gentlemen, but some had let their fame go to their heads, and they were real jerks to fly. They would demand services and fail to comply with flight attendants instructions, such as wearing their seat belts or putting up their tray tables. Some even insisted they have the same flight attendant on each flight.

We flew the band U2 around Europe for over a month, which was quite an adventure. The biggest problem we had flying rock groups was the use of drugs on the plane. We often had to threaten to not fly unless they ceased their use. It was a serious concern because the government could confiscate any airplane where illegal drugs were being used. Clay Lacy lost one of his Learjets in South America on a charter trip. After landing, the customs people vacuumed his plane, and claimed they found drugs. Bye, bye, plane. He never got it back, even after several court battles. However, the president of that country now had his own Lear.

My Friend, George Ablah

George helped me understand the importance of ethics and being true to your word. We formed a great partnership.

A Long First Day

One morning some time after I had started DeBoer Aviation, I received a call in my airport office from a man introducing himself as George Ablah. He wanted to know if I could fly him to Ozona, Texas, and I said we could.

He asked how fast we could get down there because there'd been some type of explosion in his gas plant there, and he needed to be there as quickly as possible. I said we could leave as soon as he got to the airport and have him wheels down in Ozona inside an hour after that.

While my crew was readying the plane, I called my friend and attorney, Jack McInteer, and asked if he knew George Ablah. His response became a standing joke between George and Jack, because they also soon became close friends. Jack said get paid up front as George, Jack had been told, was a crook. Nothing further from the truth turned out to be the case.

True to our word; we departed Wichita and had George in Ozona less than an hour later. Thankfully, the explosion was not serious, and no one was hurt.

While still in Ozona, George's banker in St. Paul, Min-nesota, called and said he had some papers requiring George's signature. He told the banker he could be there in a couple of hours, so we wound up flying into St. Paul's Downtown Airport. George got to the bank and signed the documents before closing time. Then another call came in.

"Hello? Yes, Mr. Ablah is here. Please hold."

Turns out the third call was from someone in Atlanta informing him about a possible real estate project. We flew from Minnesota to Atlanta, George looked over the downtown bank building in question, and rather quickly, we were soon wheels up and headed back to Wichita. George later told me that it wasn't until he'd sat down to dinner with his family, he realized what he'd done. We'd gone from Wichita, Kansas, to Ozona, Texas, to St. Paul, Minnesota, to Atlanta, Georgia, and back to Wichita all in one day. Not bad!

A Good Partnership Opportunity

George had me take him on a couple more of those trips, and it was after returning from one that he said he'd like to buy our relatively new charter company. I told him I only owned 20 percent, and that Marilyn DeBoer owned the other 80. If you recall, when we first started up our charter service, Jack DeBoer's bank had prohibited him from owning any stock.

> **Building and Keeping Relationships (Reputation)**
>
> *A person is no better than their word or reputation. It takes a long time to get a good reputation and a short period of time to get a bad one.*

Though Marilyn and I became partners and had formed DeBoer Aviation, our charter operation, Jack still siphoned off any money I was able to make from the charter business. He then used it to fund his real estate ventures.

George convinced Jack to sell 40 percent of Marilyn's stock to him, making the ownership Marilyn: 40%; George, 40%; and myself with the remaining 20%. The money for the stock went to Jack, so now Jack, George, and I were partners.

George told me he thought Jack De-Boer had one of the brightest real estate minds he'd ever encountered, and if the two of them could work together, the sky was literally the limit. Sadly, such would not turn out to be the case.

George began using our Lear a lot, but always paid for his trips. When Jack used it, he charged everything, never paying. George had Jack consult on a couple of George's real estate deals he'd had in the works. Those two men had such towering egos, it became apparent that getting them working as a team was like trying to mix oil and water.

After a couple of months of this professional dissonance, Jack came into my office and announced we were going to,

From left: George Ablah, Ron Ryan and Virginia Ablah

"Buy out that SOB's interest." Trying to slow things down a little, I politely asked him how we could make that happen. He said we'd just have to sell off some of 'our' assets to pay George off.

I was hurt, and I was honest. I told Jack his plan was lousy, and terribly unfair, considering I'd worked so many long, hard hours to build up our charter service. He didn't want to hear it, loudly asserting that either George had to go, or he would.

Ever try to be respectful while begging?

Jack's demands were the last thing I wanted, and when he realized that I wouldn't agree, he abruptly stood up, cursed me and accused me of 'doing this' because George had money and he didn't.

Nothing was further from the truth; I admired Jack and his family. They were mostly very good to me, and treated me like part of the family. I believe I returned that esteem and trust; yet, I still believe to this day, Jack DeBoer is the one who betrayed our trust. In my estimation, he'd 'done this' to himself. When he stormed out of my office that day, he slammed my door so hard the pictures jumped off the wall.

The upshot of it all is that George paid Jack for the other 40 percent of our charter's stock, leaving George with 80% of it and me with my 20%. George then said his only reason for buying the company in the first place was to have convenient, safe air travel. He said he wanted us to be equal partners, and gave me another 30%. He also said I could build up our charter service all I wanted, as long as he was able to fly as often as he needed, and do it safely. George turned out to be a great partner, and a close personal friend.

ABKO

George would chase deals anywhere in the country, as he was gifted in quickly sizing up the possibilities for commercial real estate. His specialty was taking over bank-repossessed inventory and selling it. He said his motto was, "I take someone else's turkey and turn it into a peacock." That wasn't idle boasting, either. I watched him do this often, and he turned over a billion dollars' worth of real estate, several years in a row.

ABKO was one of his biggest deals. ABKO, which stands for Ablah and Koch, was a collaborative effort between George and Charles Koch, head of Koch Industries, America's largest privately held corporation. George knew Chrysler Motor Company under Lee

From left: George and Virginia Ablah, Renae and Ron Ryan (2007)

Iacocca was in severe financial straits and had been talking to the government about a bailout.

George told me he figured that with all the real estate Chrysler owned or controlled, he and Charles could make $50 million each, on the deal. They proceeded to form ABKO and bought all of Chrysler Corporation's real estate. They then sold back to Chrysler what they needed, then sold the rest to other buyers. At the end of two years, George and Charles split $100 million dollars.

Vegas with George

George also loved to gamble, so we flew to Las Vegas a lot. He was treated well at the International Hilton, and I, as his pilot, was treated equally well. Virginia, his wife, loved attending the various shows, and the Hilton always had top entertainers like Elvis, Vic Damone, Frankie Avalon, Frank Sinatra, Liberace, and a whole lot of others.

These shows were always sold out, but I knew both the pit boss and the man who controlled the seating. I'd give him fifty dollars, and we'd always have front-row seats with complimentary meals included. Virginia has more than one of Elvis's scarves he'd drape around a pretty woman's neck sometime during his show, as Virginia was more than pretty.

For him, everything needed to be the best. That was how George rolled.

He was a colorful character, a workaholic who drank several pots of black coffee each day. He kept a suite at the Waldorf Astoria Hotel, as well as his own private limo and driver. George received excellent service wherever he went because he was a gracious and generous tipper. He knew that if you treat everyone as you want to be treated, especially service staff, they remember you. We always stayed at the Waldorf Astoria, too, and got the same tremendous service because they knew we were with George.

Unfortunately, George had another habit that was as bad as the other was good – he was a serious smoker. I finally talked him into going to the Pritikin Health Institute in California to kick that habit. While there, they twice caught him smoking, and he was asked to leave. He did manage to beg his way back in later, when he firmly promised he would quit. Thank God, he meant it and did that time. It would be another year before his wife, Virginia, kicked that habit.

Artfully Speaking

After I had been in the business for a while, George Ablah bought a Gulfstream II (G-II) and based it at our FBO. Around the same time he had purchased the G-II, he had also bought a very large complex in the NYC area, which he called the Blue Hills project. He had also purchased a lot of Henry Moore's art. Between the complex and the art, a lot of New Yorkers were attracted. He also placed a lot of high priced art in his plane. It was hard to convince some people to drill holes in the bottom of an original such as an extremely valuable *Coming Through the Rye* statue so it would meet FAA crash stress requirements. But not George; this is what he wanted, and what he did.

George also had a lot of art at his Wichita home, but he didn't think many people knew about it. One night, the neighbor's silent alarm went off; the police mistakenly thought it was George's home and responded. George's young hired help, who lived in the pool house, almost got shot when he came out to see what was going on. When the police told George everyone knew about his art collection, he didn't want his family or young kids at the time, to be compromised so he arranged with Christies in NYC to auction off about $10 million worth of his art. He brought the art out to the FBO and we loaded it into one of my Lears. I hired an armed guard to watch over the plane that night; and the next day I flew it to NYC, where it eventually was auctioned. Talk about a nervous night and flight!

Water Contamination

One of George's many real estate deals was purchasing the huge Western Electric Hawthorne plant and surrounding area in Chicago. He had sold off several sections when a buyer who wanted a major section decided they wanted to do their own ground water testing. George had done this, but they wanted to do their own. They went deeper than the people George had hired and found major water contamination; 30 to 40 feet below his test. This happened at the same time there was such controversy about ground pollution, and laws had been passed where there was no corporate veil of protection on pollution cases. The liability was unlimited, and it put George into bankruptcy.

George handled the situation well, but it took quite a toll on his wife.

George's misfortune worked in the long run, financially well for me. George was still a genius at real estate but restricted by this hiccup, as to what he could do financially. By the time this had happened, I was pretty solid, financially. So I backed George in several large real estate deals, all of which worked out very well for both of us.

The Emery Air Freight Saga

In 1977, Kay Cohlmia, a native Wichitan living in Dallas, Texas, called me. I was interested because he was related to George Ablah, my friend and partner. Cohlmia wanted to know if I was willing to fly three Cessna Citations for Emery Air Freight five nights a week, operating from several satellite hubs, to their new central overnight delivery facility being set up in Smyrna, Tennessee.

Nothing Ventured, Nothing Gained

Emery had decided to enter the overnight small-parcel express market to compete with entrepreneur Fred Smith's Federal Express. FedEx had gotten off the ground in 1973 and had a rocky financial start. By '76, Federal Express was in the black again, but Emery thought they saw an air leak and felt the competition was worth pursuing. Since FedEx

was using Falcon 20s for their startup, Kay Cohlmia was suggesting Citations instead.

I agreed, as long as the money flowed through our company and not Kay's. He agreed, and although Emery thought the pay arrangement strange, they also agreed. We started this venture with one of Kay's Citations and one of mine. I leased the third. Emery was ready and wanted to sign a 90-day contract to assess how well the Cessna's would work and I didn't want to lose that deal!

I don't recall telling anybody I liked jumping hurdles, but there sure seemed to be some set up almost from the get-go. In order to land this initial contract, Emery needed to unload 14 twin-engine Cessna Titans. I understood the aircraft weren't the issue, but that Emery had received rotten support and customer service from Cessna and

Emery Fleet of Cessna Citations

57

wanted nothing more to do with that company unless they abruptly changed their ways.

The second hurdle was that I needed to start in 60 days, which meant dealing with both of those issues immediately. No problem, right? At that time, there was a three-year backlog for new Citations, which made even buying a used one difficult.

I told Emery I knew Cessna honcho Russ Meyer and would do what I could to intercede. When I explained this all to Russ, he immediately had a package prepared to send them. The Cessna mailroom used FedEx to send the package! When it arrived at Emery Air Freight, there just happened to be a photographer right there to snap some embarrassing shots of FedEx delivering the stuff to Emery Air! Yeah. I never did find out whether it was intentional or luck on FedEx's part, although it sure seemed a little too convenient to me. But it almost kicked the entire Citation deal right in the noggin.

A New Deal

About six months later, Kay called. Emery Air Freight was giving us a 30-day notice because the Citation as configured, didn't carry enough freight. I asked if I could go talk to them. Kay agreed but mentioned he didn't want to fly for them any longer since he was working on a United States Postal Service contract. I immediately headed for Dayton, where Emery was located, spoke with Jim Reeves and Charlie Carson, and ended up with an additional three-year conditional contract using eight aircraft.

I got the contract, and now I had to deal with the condition of the jets. I needed to reconfigure the Citations to carry more packages per plane or find a reasonable alternative. During this whole process, I assessed the King Air 200, along with the Merlin turboprop aircraft. By modifying the Citation cargo netting as well as squeezing more cargo space out of the hellhole – our nickname for the extreme rear compartment of the plane – we found the Citations could carry more than any other small corporate jet or reliable turboprop.

I convinced the FAA we could use the side window and a crash axe as the required second emergency exit. This was because, in the Citation, the other emergency exit was immediately across from the main access door, which left considerable cubic space unusable.

Our sales manager, Doug Jackson, brought all fourteen of the Cessna Titans back to Wichita to sell. They were still boldly painted in Emery Air Freight's livery, so we wanted to have them repainted. Emery said they weren't going to invest any more money in those aircraft, but suggested we include in any sales contract that the buyer had to remove the name.

Shortly thereafter, one morning the phone rang. It was a reporter asking if it was true that Emery Air Freight really would carry anything, anywhere, anytime. They knew something I didn't; somebody had used one of these aircraft to haul a load of marijuana.

The plane had crashed in Texas. The pilot managed to get out and escape the law, but we found out he'd fueled the plane and charged the fuel to Emery. The next day those planes were having all mention of Emery Air Freight removed.

Nearing the end of our three-year contract, Emery said they wanted to begin using larger aircraft. Since we had the best on-time record, and since they'd decided to adopt the motto, "We Will Fly Anything, Anywhere, Anytime," we no longer had further need for the Citations. Emery asked us to help them with due diligence in choosing the best transport aircraft for their needs.

With the assistance of Doug Jackson and Boeing's Lionel Alford, Emery looked at the 737 before settling on the Boeing 727. The 727s were not only plentiful; many of them already were outfitted with cargo doors.

Though the 737 was initially cheaper to operate with only two engines and not requiring a flight engineer, cargo planes aren't flown as frequently as commercial airliners. We were fortunate that Boeing had such an imposing influence in Wichita. They provided us with extensive comparison data allowing us to make an informed decision between the two aircraft. For Emery, the 727 was a better choice even though it had three engines and required three crew members. Each freighter, although it had two crews assigned to it, flew only about 100 hours a month, while the airlines flying anything less than 250 hours a month was considered low utilization.

Next, Emery asked if we wanted to bid on five of the twenty 727s they planned to either buy or contract out. I expected this request, but knew in order to fly this type of aircraft, we needed to hold an FAA Part 121 airline certificate.

Super. We held only a Part 135 certificate. We went ahead and bid, anyway, for which Emery awarded us a three-year contract for five B-727s providing we could be saddled up and ready to ride in 90 days. No pressure. We could get over this hurdle.

We haunted both local and regional FAA offices in Kansas City, begging them to help us make this happen. Their response?

"Impossible!" They said at that time they were in the process of certifying the Boeing 757 for TWA, also located in Kansas City, and simply couldn't add our request to the mix.

It so happens that in Denver right at the same time, United Airlines had a bunch of pilots furloughed. The Denver FAA office was looking for work, and said they were available to help us any way they could, and they'd get started just as soon as we moved our operations to Denver.

It helps to know people. After I thought about our di-

> ### Building Enterprises and Entrepreneurialism
>
> *Always look for new opportunities. Always find the service or product that the public wants or needs; and once you have that, building it cheaper or better. In other words, try to either build a better mousetrap or one that sells for less money.*

lemma for a few minutes, I called Bob Dole's office and told them to show our forwarding address as Denver. Astonished, they asked why. When I laid the whole thing out for them, they told me to just hold the phone until they could make a few calls.

The following week, we had our very own full-time FAA certification expert in our office whose orders were to stay with us until we got our Part 121 certificate. Sixty days from that date, we had it! We resubmitted our bid to Emery, and they awarded us five 727s to fly for them.

We then needed flight crews, and quickly. In airline training, it doesn't make any difference if you have flown for another airline in the same type of plane; you must go through the new airline's full training program. During that period, United Airlines had many furloughed B-727 pilots. We went to United and told them we would hire some of those pilots to fly with our new guys, and when or if United wanted them back, they could go if they chose. We also agreed to use United's training facilities and their flight simulators located in Denver.

This stroke of luck worked well for everyone, as United would rather see their pilots flying than sitting around, plus we started using some of their maintenance support in San Francisco. We had our own training and maintenance program set up but used the United's facilities to train our pilots alongside the furloughed United pilots. Timing in life can play a critical role in one's success.

The First Airline 1980-1986

Ryan International Airlines was added in 1980, when we started flying big airplanes.

Ryan International Airlines

When we received our first Boeing 727 for Emery in 1980, we based it in Wichita. I remember it like it was last night. When a friend, Boeing test and corporate pilot, Ken Gephardt flew it in from Seattle, weather minimums were a definite factor, and we were covered with the dense fog, often common in our area. However, from my upper-story airport office window, I could see the stars and knew the fog was a thin blanket. I stayed in radio contact with Ken over Unicom, and he decided that under Part 191 flight rules, he could opt to shoot the approach. He did, landing without incident.

An immediate issue arose, we needed care and feeding for our big plane and the rest of its kin. At that time, TWA was providing maintenance and turnaround services for most, if not all the air carriers serving Wichita's Mid-Continent Airport. My first move was to meet with them, asking for their quote to provide the standard de-icing, lavatory, galley, cleaning and normal maintenance services.

Their response was to bring in their top union representative, who oversaw the entire 15-man Wichita maintenance crew. The minute he found out we weren't union

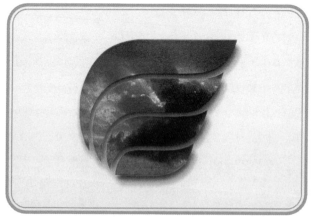

Ryan International Logo

he said, "Sorry, nothin' personal. Can't help you." They refused to help us in any way.

Early in our FBO days I had hired our chief of maintenance, Ray Thomas, from Cessna Aircraft Company. He was a vital part of the FBO and both airlines. I bought a de-icing truck, an aircraft transport tug, and all the anticipated support equipment we'd need to take care of our 727. We then found the two best and most experienced maintenance men available and hired them.

Our little operation was working so nicely, it raised some eyebrows. First, United Airlines' Billie Ulick asked for a quote to service her planes transiting Wichita. I reasoned it to be a good use of the men and equipment I'd invested in, so I agreed. That worked so well that Continental's Bob Becker wanted in. Again, I said yes.

You're probably ahead of me. According to our customers, it wasn't long before our two-man crew was steadily providing better, more consistent service than the 10 to 15-man crew from the union run shop!

You might recall my younger-year experiences with the way unions did things. I'm not castigating every union, nor painting all union reps and shop stewards with the same brush, because some of them do solid work and have strong reputations. But, under the Transport Workers Union rules I'm talking about here, a union tug driver wasn't allowed to do anything else, the man riding the brakes couldn't check the oil, and the stupidity just rolled on, while the service got poorer.

As our airline maintenance operation kept growing, we needed more space. Wichita's airport, like most, would not allow businesses to own field property. They were willing to lease ground space and let us build some nice hangars for them. But the titles remained in their name, and after a set amount of years we got the "blessing" of paying rent on buildings we put up in the first place. The only positive there is that we paid no property taxes, and the airport did not require any financial support from either the city of Wichita or Sedgwick County.

United Parcel Service

We had been flying for Emery Air Freight for some time when the phone rang. It was United Parcel Service (UPS) informing us they were buying ten 727-200s and wanted us to give them a price to fly them. They had been monitoring our performance for Emery and liked what they saw.

I didn't expect Emery to like it. Besides, I'd signed an agreement to not fly for any of their competitors. They didn't, and at first turned me down flat. Knowing that would be the case, I had given some thought to the business end of it, coming up with a few ideas – one of which was how cost-effective it would be for me to operate 15 Boeing 727s as opposed to just the five they already had. Emery thought it made sense and changed their tune.

We added the extra ten planes with no issues, other than needing to eventually replace the lame 'new and improved' fuel monitoring systems the -200s had on them. We fliers all agreed: when flying long distances in questionable or marginal weather, it's a real good idea to know how much fuel is in the tank. After all, as our Air Force friends like to say, "Sometime, somewhere, whether you want to or not, you will land." I've always preferred making that decision myself.

Shortly, Emery called again, asking if we could handle a few more 727s currently being flown by an unpopular operator. The short version is that we wound up flying 22 Boeing 727s for Emery Air Freight and ten more for UPS. What I'm trying to say is, we managed to stay busy.

Business was brisk. We soon outgrew the FBO at the airport and ended up leasing the entire fifth floor of one of George Ablah's downtown buildings – the old Farm

Emery's and United Parcel Service's Boeing 727s

61

Credit Bank. That is where our headquarters remained until 1986, when we sold it to Peterson, Heather & Howell (PHH).

UPS had told us even before we began flying for them, they eventually wanted to operate their own in-house airline. We agreed from day one that we'd support that. We even went so far as to offer them the use of all our maintenance, training and ops books whenever they felt they were ready to take that on. UPS was then and remains one great company. They weren't shy in making demands, but they were always fair when they made them.

As we flew for them, they kept asking us to do things outside our contract with them. We got to talking about it and one day called them, saying we thought we should be compensated for all the extra-curricular tasks.

"Okay, how much?"

I told them, "One million more per year." They said they'd send their time study specialists out to assess our claim, which they promptly did. When the study was complete, UPS got back to us and said they agreed we'd been consistently accomplishing non-contractual duties, but they disagreed as to how much more we should be paid for them.

I thought, "Well, here it comes. Go ahead and drop the other boot." Imagine my shock when they said, "According to our findings, we should be paying you two million dollars more per year for all the extra stuff you've been doing for us." We'd have been satisfied with what we initially asked for, but we didn't argue the point. Talk about a fantastic company!

Our ongoing relationship was such that we eventually put Boeing's first five right-out-of-the-box cargo-specialized 757s into service with them. We worked diligently to maintain an excellent relationship with both Emery and UPS. Even in Emery's early start-up years when most companies – and Emery was one of them – have financial growing pains, they still always paid us on time, every time. On one occasion, I agreed to forgo any profits for three months to help with Emery's financial woes. That paid back handsomely over the years. Being up front, pre-cise and offering the best services around, paid off for Ryan International Airlines and our customers. I recommend those practices to anyone determined to be successful.

Passenger Service Changed Our Deal

We started our FAA Part 121 freight operation with B-727 aircraft in 1980, and in 1983 we leased/purchased two Boeing 727-100s for passenger service. We had signed a three-year contract with Tom Wainwright, who was head of an East Coast travel agency specializing in flying people to warm-weather destinations during winter, and to gambling casinos and other locations during summer.

That was our first adventure working with a travel agent who not only sold retail travel packages to the public himself, but also sold wholesale packages to other travel agencies. It was an education. Getting Department of Transportation (DOT) approval was a bureaucratic nightmare.

DOT honcho Dan McKinney wanted my partner, George Ablah, to produce audited financial statements. George didn't hand out his financial statements to anyone; personal, audited, or otherwise. Anyway, the nature of a personal financial statement makes having an audited copy impossible. After untangling that mess, we barely got started in time to organize the first trips, and that soured George on the entire passenger side of business. He still agreed we should proceed growing the passenger business but wanted me to find a way to buy him out, using either a public offering or a cash/stock deal.

That's when I sought out Jack McInteer to help me by becoming president of the Arline, and I took the Chairman of the board position. Bringing in Jack was one of my better decisions, as he did an excellent job getting our financial statements and business model positioned for either an IPO or a sale.

As luck would have it, we identified two buyers competing to purchase our company. One, led by a former GE executive named Stanger, wanted a leveraged buyout; while the other, Peterson, Heather & Howell (PHH), a publicly traded company, offered cash/stock. In order to get the best price for our airline, we needed good financial records. Jack brought Derry Larsons' accounting firm on board, and we have worked and become friends with Derry and Kay since that time.

Peterson, Heather & Howell is based in Hunt Valley, Maryland. They specialize in fleet financing and had already been working with UPS, so we thought the sale would go smoothly and our employees would have a better future, if we went with them.

Then, too, we'd always been intentional in taking care of our company employees. Though PHH's offer was a couple million dollars less than the other, we'd been providing our employees with a 401k plan and felt PHH would take better care of them. The PHH deal was less risky for our people than the leveraged buyout Stanger was offering. The offer from PHH was all cash via a stock transaction, requiring us to hold onto that stock for a minimum of six months. We sold the company to PHH in June of 1986.

With the sale, George was paid his share, and so was I. However, we continued working together doing real estate deals. Things worked so well that when George was able to get his own financing again, he elected to keep me in on his real estate purchases. Up until, and even after George died, I was still reaping profits from some of those deals. In all the deals we did together, we never had a loss. George had a full-time real estate person working for him named Frank Mills. Frank was, and is, a super detail guy, and nice to boot; when Frank talked, we listened, and he remains a friend to me today.

George Ablah, My Partner

Watching George interact with people and put business deals together was quite an education. He was also very generous with real estate brokers. So, when they found a good deal, they would call George, first. One year, each one of the top ten salesmen for Coldwell Banker all worked with George.

A man of his word, if George promised something, you could count on it happening. Very few people have the privilege of having close friends in their lifetime. When I think about really close friends, George was a unique in-

dividual in a positive way. My friend and partner, George, died a few years ago, and I miss him. Virginia lived in a senior assisted-living complex with her two dogs and unfortunately, recently passed away.

My partnership with George helped me establish financial security and I acquired a good friend as well. A good friend is more valuable than gold...and I am blessed with several people I can call good friends.

George Ablah and Ron Ryan

63

In the Interim and the Second Airline

Selling the airline freed up a lot of time, and also created new opportunities and adventures. I had to find something to do with my time. Still bound by my non-compete aviation clause, I tried hot air! Dabbling in real estate lead me to meet my wife, Renae. Witnessing what those rascals had done to my airline, after two years, I couldn't help myself; I jumped back in; and together, we built the second airline. I'm getting ahead of myself, so please continue the ride with me...

Ryan International Milestones

1978 – 30 Day start up of 8 Cessna Citations

1981 – 60 Day Conversion of Certificate from 135 to 121

1984 – Operated First 8 B–727–200 Freight Aircraft

1984 – Operated 3 B–727 PAX Aircraft

1987 – Operated Frist B–757 Freight Aircraft

1989 – 60 Day Start up of 8 DC–9 Aircraft

1989 – 16 Day Start up of 9 B–727–100 Aircraft

1990 – 14 Day Start up of 25 B–727–100 Aircraft

1991 – One Week Implementation of DNET Operation

Director, Division of Aviation

Secretary of Transportation

WEEK OF APRIL 9, 1990 — WICHITA BUSINESS JOURNAL

PROFILE

Ron Ryan

Relative newcomer to city joins pre-eminent group of aviation entrepreneurs

By TAMI BRADLEY

Ryan Aviation Corporation

WICHITA
Company Picnic

SATURDAY
JUNE 27, 1992
2:00 PM – ?
Dinner Served at 5:00 PM

1847 WELLINGTON PLACE
WICHITA, KANSAS

RSVP 946-4990
by JUNE 22

Please bring your lawn
chairs,
towels and appetite

---

28   THE WICHITA EAGLE-BEACON   Monday, September 26, 1988

Pilot buys back brainchild
after its business declines

Ryan Aviation wants to corner carrier services

Q&A
With
Ron Ryan

"Our goal is
have fun, make
money while
we're doing it
and have our
people make
money."
— Ron Ryan

The Argentinean Adventure

Anyone who knows me knows my love of aviation. That, coupled with my non-compete clause, caused me a lot of frustration. Although I was working a few real estate deals, aviation was still my passion. I needed to keep busy, but doing what?

A Hot Air Balloon, of Course

Our goal was to complete the first round-the-world nonstop hot air balloon flight!

My friend, who I've mentioned before, former Air National Guard Commander Rowland Smith, who goes by Smitty, was also a hot air balloon enthusiast. He'd taken me with him to Albuquerque, New Mexico, several times to fly with him in the hot air balloon festival. The topography there is such that it's possible to lift off, fly at one altitude in one direction, and then rise to catch the winds aloft going the opposite direction. The whole idea is to spend hours aloft that way, yet still land very close to where you launched.

In 1987, when Smitty found out I was available, he asked if I'd help him and a Kansas City friend make the first around-the-world flight in a hot air balloon. After a few nanoseconds of debate, I eagerly agreed, and the planning began.

Through his military service connections, Smitty arranged for an Air Force C-130 to fly both balloons and all necessary equipment, including a nitrogen-generating station, to our launch point in Mendoza, Argentina. One was the hot air balloon,

Colonel Rowland Smith, Jr. (Smitty)

and the second was a hydrogen weather balloon, capable of flying substantially higher than a hot air balloon; it was mounted above the hot air balloon.

Smitty and his partner had modified a nuclear waste capsule as their pressurized gondola, equipped with all necessary communications and navigation systems. They'd also modified the hot air balloon burner to use both propane and another gas because of the much higher altitudes at which we would be flying.

My primary duty was to set up the surprisingly large nitrogen generating station. Not only would we fill the weather balloon with it; but at higher altitudes, nitrogen is often needed to help boost the propane up through the lines to the burner, so we needed to have it with us. We couldn't exactly set down just anywhere and say, "Pardon me, but would you happen to have some grey nitrogen?"

They told me only after we'd left United States airspace, I was the backup pilot. They must've understood I didn't have the FAA-required pilot certificate specifying the rating of "lighter-than-air free balloon" needed for hot air balloon operations in the US I guess those two were operating under the guideline that it's easier to ask forgiveness than to seek permission.

We were going to launch from the military base in Mendoza, Argentina. The jet stream was stronger there, and there was less land mass, which eliminated some potential turbulence and weather problems such as thunderstorms.

On the way south, we made a fuel stop in Panama, planning to stay at a downtown hotel. Upon arriving, the Air Force wouldn't let us off base because the operation to capture Manuel Noriega had commenced. We enjoyed base housing instead, and took off the next morning for Argentina.

Since we were staging from the Mendoza military base, everyone was on edge because of the just-lost battle with Britain over the Falkland Islands or, as everyone cautioned us to call them, Islas Malvinas. The locals were very touchy about being called anything else.

> *"If there's more than one way to do a job and one of those ways will end in disaster, then somebody will do it that way."*
> *-Captain Edward J Murphy, Jr*

For the first few days there, the Argentinian military personnel were professionally courteous, but distant. My charm and Smitty's smarts must've rubbed off on them, because it wasn't long before things warmed up and we started having the good-natured fun shared by enlisted military men the world over. Even their officers joined in. I found it interesting that their commanding general told me, after we had become friends, they all knew challenging Britain was a losing deal; that they'd get their butts kicked, and the whole thing was crazy, but politics ruled over good sense. Seems like that is still true, even here and now.

Preparations for our anticipated flight were going on during the whole time. Smitty had gotten us a satellite communications system, normally strictly for military use. So, each day we'd set up our small dish, locate the proper satellite, and talk with Offutt AFB outside of Omaha, Nebraska. Remember, this was long before cell phones.

All told, we spent almost a month readying everything and monitoring the weather. Our desire was to launch just ahead of a weather front moving through. On the ground, the weather balloon was paper-thin and fragile. It couldn't take much blowing around. Once airborne, though, it would give with any shifting winds aloft.

Great news! We finally got the weather we needed. I revved up the nitrogen generator and started filling the weather balloon while the other two went to get the hot air balloon tanks filled. We'd made previous arrangements for the right blended fuel, but ol' Murphy showed up.

The man filling the tanks used straight propane and it blew out all of the seals, requiring extensive repairs. By the time the repairs were done, and the tanks were properly filled, we were watching the weather front go over. The weather balloon was shredded, along with our hopes to complete the first round-the-world nonstop hot air balloon flight.

That trip was not for the faint of heart! Only after two failed attempts, Bertrand Piccard of Switzerland and Brian Jones of Great Britain, finally pulled it off in the Breitling Orbiter 3, in March of 1999.

Not to Be

I still believe we could have done it.

At any rate, Argentina is a beautiful country, so we chose to do some sightseeing while there. On one such trip, we stopped at a quaint little mountainside café. We decided to set up our satellite antenna beside the road to chat with Offutt and let them know what was happening.

As it turns out, a little more had happened than we knew. Apparently, some folks thought we were spies and called the police. They quickly surrounded us, and we found ourselves staring down gun barrels. A lot of them.

Following some language interpretation, they let us go. And that, friends, was Ron and Smitty's excellent adventure that almost got off the ground!

The Second Airline 1988-2004

A man can't dedicate over 20 years of his life to a worthy endeavor and watch it crumble. PHH had some political foolishness going on and I had to do something about it!

Speaking of Murphy

We didn't know until after the sale what political games had been going on behind the scenes. The nutshell version is that PHH's president had vacated to become chairman, and two of their oldest bull elk wanted to be its new president, with all the love, mutual esteem and fairness such a power play reveals.

As the story goes, the one chosen to be the new president called the loser up to his new corner-office digs and asked him what he'd like to be and do for PHH. That man, still smarting at not being selected, said he thought PHH should be in the aviation business. The new honcho and board said to go for it, so he did. He bought an FAA Part 135 charter company; an aircraft credit card company; an aircraft consulting company—and his last acquisition was our FAA Part 121 airline and FBO.

Please understand before the sale, our on-time performance was so good we had other wholesale companies wanting us to bid on flying some of their routes. We did, and eventually wound up with another lease/purchase of a 727-200 we outfitted with 189 seats to fit a customer's request. When we got the plane, there was no interior except a throne right in the middle, mounted on a rotating platform that always had whoever sat in it facing to the east. I figured it belonged to some humble person like the New York Governor or Bill Belichick but, alas, it was for a well-heeled Muslim who always wanted to be facing east while his guests sat on the floor.

During the process of getting FAA approval to operate this aircraft, they asked for floor loading specifications to ensure it was structurally sound enough to handle 189 passenger seats. Only Boeing could provide that information, but they said it would cost us at least fifty thousand dollars and take six months to complete. We had to do something, and fast.

I had previously worked with Boeing's Lionel Alford and Bev Lancaster when selecting the proper aircraft for Emery's initial B-727 fleet, so I reached out to Bev. He just happened to be in Seattle at the time, so he had one of his engineers work one entire weekend. The following Monday, Bev had the data to us that the FAA required – and neither he nor Boeing ever charged us a dollar for the work. He and that unknown engineer literally saved our company!

I add these facts to point out how diligent we'd been to maintain excellent relationships with contractors, suppliers, and clients right from the start.

It seems the minute Peterson, Heather & Howell (PHH), gained control of what had been our company, they began treating long-time FBO customers like they weren't important – and those customers began moving away in droves.

Under our guidelines, whenever UPS would call and want to meet, we'd usually fly down that very day, or no later than the following day. When they'd call PHH, it would often take weeks just to meet. After a year of that, UPS said they were done and began the process of recovering their plane under their new air carrier certificate.

This didn't set well with me. It hadn't even been a year since our sale to PHH, yet they were poised to lose their biggest customer. Friends at Emery told me they were just as disgusted by PHH's service. The good news? Most of our B-727 and B-757 pilots were hired by UPS and several have now retired, very well off, from their experience. Several also moved into important management divisions of the then new UPS airline.

Anyway, I was stymied. I'd signed a three year non-competition agreement with PHH, and they were real asses about holding me to its terms of doing nothing that was aviation related. Even when I was asked by a wealthy developer if I would help develop a general aviation runway in Breckenridge, Colorado, PHH turned me down flat. They said they would sue me if I pursued the project. Nice guys. In retrospect, I now know it was because they knew they didn't know what they were doing; and they knew I did.

Repurchasing the FBO

After almost two years of observing those wannabes systematically loot and pillage the FBO we'd kept in such great condition, I made an offer to buy it back at considerably less than the offer I'd earlier tried to get them to consider. They evidently saw the handwriting in my expression, and this time they took the deal. That was a good thing because I wasn't playing around. I was buying back the FBO at that time, for pennies on the dollar.

Arrogance and ignorance have destroyed many a fine company.

The respite was short-lived. By the time they flew into Wichita to sell me back the FBO, the arrogance had returned. They were overbearing and unkind. Throughout

the closing, they kept emphasizing, "What you see is what you get; if it isn't here, you don't own it. If you see it and it belongs to PHH, you own it." After hearing that several times, part of me sat back and began wondering what that was about, and I thought of a response.

When everyone had signed and they were stretching and picking up their briefcases to leave, I casually asked how they were planning on getting home. They looked at me like I had a third ear and said, "In that PHH jet parked right out there on the ramp. Why?"

"You just told me three or four times that, according to the contract we all just signed, anything belonging to PHH I could see is now ours." Their lawyers about swallowed their gizzards and acted like they were having heart problems.

I didn't let them off for a while, but finally chuckled and told them I was having fun at their expense. You could almost hear the air swooshing back into the room. PHH had evidently pulled that one before and figured we'd be intimidated. But we weren't.

Even though I smiled at them, I didn't feel it inside. I – all of us – had all of their rough manners we were going to take. We disliked them and what they'd done to the company.

A very short time after PHH left Kansas and were back in Maryland, I made a bare-bones offer to buy back the airline. They whined about how much they'd paid previously for the airline and how little I was offering.

Ron Ryan had some fun during a recent press conference, showing that he was "reclaiming" the FBO he sold in 1986 to PHH Aviation.

Ron Ryan removing PHH letters on FBO

Repurchasing the Airline

I just waited . . .

It only took a month. We all knew PHH would accept my offer because I'd done my due diligence. The only thing left was the FAA air carrier certificate, fax machine and a typewriter. I had the FBO campus to help rebuild the airline at the same time, which made sense to me. I had to hustle, though. PHH had lost every one of their planes. They only had two remaining employees, Jeff Crippen and Ray Thomas; and the local FAA wanted to pick up their Part 121 operating certificate. The repurchase of the airline did not require that they come back to Wichita, which was good. The lawyers handled the sale and we went our separate ways.

Finding Planes

The day following our buyback of the airline, I called Chuck Zubarik at Emery Air Freight, wanting to know if he had some planes that

Back in business with Ryan Aviation

I could lease to keep our air carrier certificate. He said we were in luck, as they'd just bought Purolator Corporation, which owned nine DC-9s. Emery had a long term plan to use them to seek a future contract with the U. S. Postal Service flying mail.

Chuck had one of those DC-9s flown to Wichita the next day under the pretense of doing audio work. I signed a lease for a dollar a month, and took the lease to our local FAA office, and the certificate issue was solved. Once again, it really does help to have friends and maintain relationships.

Shortly thereafter, Chuck came out to Wichita, asking if we'd be interested in flying some 727s being operated by Orion Airlines. He said they weren't performing up to standards and they wanted to fire them if we could start flying the planes Emery had leased to them. We had everything in place to run those aircraft, so I said "Yes, of course!"

We negotiated a contract on a Big Chief notebook and wrote it out on a cocktail napkin over coffee. We got everyone's signatures and began planning!

He'd no sooner gotten home when Chuck called wanting to know if he could back out of our contract. He felt really squeezed because Orion had been yelling for a substantial pay raise and they were threatening to go out on strike if Emery replaced them, effectively shutting down the whole operation.

Of course, I said we'd let them out of our contract. Little did I know at the time, we would eventually get all of the planes as long as we could have them flying within 30 days of receipt. Chuck and Emery were grateful that we did not push the fact they had a signed contract with us. He said they were bidding on a major USPS contract which, if landed, they'd want us to fly their DC-9s, while Emery would fly the 727s, along with a DC-8 they'd acquired with the purchase of a small startup California airline.

My Management Philosophy

I think our airline people liked to get me out of the office, so they could get their jobs done without me watching over their shoulder. I really liked that. I had a management philosophy that was very simple:

1. Make sure the employees know what their jobs are. A job description no more than two pages is essential. If the job changes, then change the job description.
2. Very important: Give them the authority to carry out that job.
3. Monitor that they are doing one and two. It's that simple.

Where most managers fail is not allowing the worker to carry out his or her assignments/authority without interference or permission.

If I had someone come into my office and ask me how to do something, I would ask them why I needed them. I always welcomed their asking for my opinion as long as they had their own solution to their, not my, problem. If I had someone try to 'blame' someone else, I would stop everything and get everyone involved in the same room to hear all sides of the story. Amazing how that stopped a lot of accusations between workers. I did have the best employees in the world. They were family to me, and for the most part, each other.

Monday Morning Meetings

In the running of our airline, I held a mandatory Monday morning managers' meeting. I hate meeting for the sake of checking a box and saying we've had a meeting. Some are a waste of time, but our Monday morning meetings were anything but.

All department managers had to report what their department had done the previous week, and we compared that to what they had told us the week before that they were going to accomplish. It was called accountability, and it kept everybody sharp.

There were no excuses for missing a meeting, short of a family emergency. Occasionally, someone would need to be out of town, but knew any scheduled meeting could not be on Monday mornings. We accomplished a lot in these meetings. The secretaries would often hear us yelling and shouting at each other; worried about what was going on. Then one of us would poke our head out and ask if they would have lunch sent in.

Our goal was to discuss any issues impacting safety or performance. Sometimes those discussions resembled knock-down, drag-out arguments; but once the discussion was over, our differences had been either ironed out or plainly stated, and we all came out with a clear direction. It was amazing how well we worked together during the week. We not only acted like family but felt like family working together.

Turks and Caicos

Having just restarted our original company, we were looking for new business. We received a call from a broker representing Al Gannaway credited with popularizing "The Nashville Sound." Al had picked up a failed casino startup in the Turks and Caicos Islands, and wanted to get a Boeing 727 freight operation to those islands started. He said if we'd come down and discuss it, he'd put us up in his Club Carib.

Trying to keep costs at a minimum, I didn't want to pay extra attorney fees for the several days it would take, so I offered my attorney, Jack McInteer, a contingency fee if he'd come with me. I mean, hey, Club Carib? A possible freight operation to the Turks and Caicos? What's not to like?

Naturally, we both took our wives along . . .

You notice this section was called, "In the Interim and Second Airline." I'm reminding you of that because something else, quite significant, happened to me between the hot air balloon journey and re-acquiring my aviation enterprises…I married my lovely wife, Renae! Let's get you caught up before finishing what happened in Turks and Caicos!

Renae and I

Meeting Renae was one of the best things that ever happened to me. Being married to her completely transformed my life, and it was another example of God's great timing.

I bought a three-story office building in downtown Wichita right across from the courthouse and close to city and county halls. It was to be a full-service office for lawyers and accountants who didn't want their own full-time secretarial staff. We provided phone service, typing and filing needs or most any other office necessities. I knew whoever was to manage the facility needed to be thick skinned, smart and able to put up with the unique personalities most lawyers and accountants had.

God's Great Timing

We interviewed several people for the job, and one person who interviewed was named Renae. She was very attractive and proved to be very smart. I asked a lot of questions that either were not legal to ask or inappropriate to see how she would react.

She told me in the most polite way that I was a jerk and at that time she was right. I asked her to come to work and was pleasantly surprised when she agreed. She avoided me as much as she could at the office but handled her job as office manager extremely well. Renae, having been brought up on a Mennonite farm, loved the smell of kerosene, which is essentially jet fuel. Once I bought back the FBO and airline, she asked if she could come to work at the airport, so she could be outside and join the airline enterprise. I was glad she asked. I easily found someone to run Rental Resources, and Renae brought her administration experience, and her other skill sets and abilities to our offices. She was a perfect fit to help rebuild the airline. Her work ethic was impeccable, and besides, I enjoyed having

her near me, though she still didn't like me at the time.

The day Bill Green heard I had bought the airline back he came into Renae's office and said, "Where is Mr. Ryan? I am here to work for him again and help him get restarted!"

Bill was a tall, well-dressed guy who carried a big black briefcase and when she saw him, all Renae could say was, "Yes, sir!"

Bill had worked for me from the FBO through the first airline sale. He was an old-fashioned accountant, who used the calculator instead of computers and by this time, he was in his late 70s. She escorted him to my office and that was that. Bill worked with us until we sold the airline the second time.

One can only imagine with all of this going on our team worked day and night seven days a week to accomplish what the FAA required. Renae and I were spending so much time working together that we came to know each other well, but whenever I took her out to dinner, we always had another person in attendance, usually Bill Green.

About a year after we met, while flying the King Air on a trip to see my mother back in Burlington, with just Renae and myself on board, I asked her to marry me and she said yes. I did it then because I wanted to tell my mother I was going to marry Renae, if she said yes.

Although I have had a lot of successful days that's been my most successful one. We recently celebrated our 32nd wedding anniversary. My, how time flies.

Renae is a graduate of Friends University and is an accomplished piano player who loves to play for the Lord in church. While "dating," we went to several different churches and eventually settled in at the First Church of the Nazarene, in Wichita. The Pastor, Gene Williams, who later became one of my best friends, preached a sermon that Sunday titled, "How Churches Tend to Shoot their Wounded." Sounded like he had prepared that sermon just for us, and we knew we had found our new church home.

About a year later, Gene agreed to marry us. By the time the wedding date was closing in, Gene said he always wanted a pre-marital conference and we agreed. We had become such close friends in the meantime that when the meeting took place in his office, Gene looked a bit uncomfortable in the beginning. I think his discomfort was because there is 15-year difference in age between me and Renae.

I leaned over and said, "Gene, I know what you are going to say, but if she dies, she dies."

Ron and Renae's wedding

It took a few moments, but when he got it, he laughed. That helped ease the tension. Then he said, "The only thing I will tell the two of you is never go to bed angry with one another. There will be times you are angry but get on your knees and pray together, as it is hard to be angry and pray at the same time."

His wise counsel has worked for 32 years, but I jokingly tell my friends I am on my third set of knee pads.

Renae's dad, Harv Schmucker, another truly wonderful man of God and his wife Carrie, were not happy Renae was going to marry me. He told her I would be an old man while she was still young. He was right, but as an old man, she has kept me young. (Just recently, I had my aortic heart valve replaced, but I'm still able to keep up with her.)

We weren't certain that they would show up on our wedding day, but they did! Renae's parents came along with her sister Cindy and baby Brittany, who flew in from Colorado to join my family from Iowa; at the church Renae was ecstatic and the wedding went very well.

The next morning, Renae and I were going to fly to Hawaii for our honeymoon. We boarded the Delta airplane and shortly after, the captain announced they had a mechanical issue. We saw the Ryan mechanics show up outside, and when I talked to them, they said the fix would take more than an hour. We had a tight connection in Dallas so I had Doug Jackson get my King Air out and fly us to Dallas. As we were landing, we heard our flight to Hawaii taxing out. We got a later flight through Los Angeles, but all went well.

Club Carib Continued

Now that you're caught up, let's get back to Turks and Caicos…

Taking our wives to a tropical destination! Best-laid plans, right?!? Let's just say it was an unforgettable trip for all of us.

The plane that took us there was a weathered, gray-haired Britten-Norman Trislander; a three-engine, fixed-gear, piston-driven, narrow, uncomfortable conveyance that didn't exactly fill us with confidence.

Half the cockpit instruments were missing, the pilot was in ratty sandals and cargo shorts, and there was a used sick bag on one of the seats. When we asked what we were supposed to do with it, he shrugged and said to throw it out. I'm not ashamed to admit it. That flight was scary, even for me.

The Trislander pilot wanted to show us the sea life on the way, so he flew way too low and circled a lot. I did mention the fixed gear, right? For land? We did this pretty much all the way there.

Because Turks and Caicos Islands are actually a collection of cays (keys), we stopped at different islands to pick up and drop off both cargo and people. On our next-to-last stop, every seat was full. The pilot wanted to load a fat lady on board, in the cargo hold! I came up for air. "No way! Nuh-uh! Not happening!"

Next, they loaded a bunch of pizzas onto the co-pilot's seat. The pilot said, "You trying to kill me?" The control yoke would not go back all the way due to the pizza boxes stacked in the seat.

Ron Ryan with Airplane Wreckage
found in Turks and Caicos

I felt like I was more among a happy pirate crew than on an airline.

I couldn't help but wonder, if our flight lasted much longer, what other great adventures awaited us? I don't know how the pilot worked around the pizza boxes, but we finally got back in the air and on our way.

When we reached our destination on an outer island, a crew was unloading a large, heavy box with Caterpillar on the side, stamped on all sides with LEAD ACID BAT-TERY – THIS SIDE UP. They were rolling the heavy box across the cargo floor of that Trislander!

Hey, I'm as up for a good time as the next guy, but when it came time to leave, I told Jack I wasn't flying anywhere in that plane, even if I had to swim back, sharks or no sharks! Fortunately for us, we were able to charter a twin Aztec when we left a few days later. Renae and Sandi, Jack's wife, were extremely relieved.

Oh—and Club Carib? It was nothing more than a shack with a bar and a few dumpy rooms. At a glance, it was obvious that a freight operation such as Al Gannaway envisioned was not going to fly, not even with that forsaken Trislander; let alone a big Boeing 727.

The broker kicked sand when we turned it down, but Al offered to take us deep-sea fishing to show no hard feelings. We graciously agreed to go.

The next morning, we were greeted by barefoot Johnnie in an aluminum Jon boat, ready to take us out into a bay, well-stocked with barracuda. We couldn't get away from there fast enough! We went back to the main island and relaxed for a few days at one of the nice resorts there. We'd had all the Turks and Caicos adventures we wanted! I still rib Jack about his first (and only) contingency case with me!

All deals aren't good deals, and we weren't desperate. Happy to be back, fully engaged in the aviation industry, with my wife and partner by my side, I was confident things would work out, given a little time.

The Colorado Real Estate Deals

I had a large lot on the top of one of the mountains in Breckenridge, Colorado, where I was going to build a home.

Renae, you know, the smarter one in our family, suggested we get a condo first and see how much we would use it. We bought a nice "ski-in, ski-out," convenient to everything. Well, everything except us. Evidenced by the fact that we used it twice in two years, we now knew we weren't snow bunnies!

When the ski lift broke down, we decided to put the condo on the market. The problem was, we were on it at the time it broke; while the wind whistled around us, rocking us back and forth, and the snow was falling, us freezing and knocking icicles off our noses. Always the optimist, I asked Renae, "So, how much do you think somebody'd pay us to have this much fun?" We reached the top and skied down, put the condo on the market, and it sold in less than a week. I like the sun, the sand and the water a lot better.

For quite a while, a surgeon who had built a multimillion dollar home next to that mountaintop lot had been trying to buy that from me. Though it was still empty, I guess he wasn't crazy about neighbors. Anyway, since I had bought it years earlier, I had very little in the lot. I knew I'd take a tax hit on any sale, so I'd continually put the good doctor off.

One day Renae walked in and matter-of-factly told me she had struck a deal with the doctor and we were selling the Breckenridge lot. I was building up a good head of steam. Can you believe what some women do? Then she happened to casually mention the selling price. "Taxes? What taxes?" I might've even given her a hug. She did good; I figured I'd keep her.

Pastoral Influence

A couple of years after Gene Williams had performed our wedding ceremony, I got a call from Gene's family saying Betty, Gene's wife had just died. They were on a trip to the East Coast when it happened. She woke up with a headache and died shortly after, from a brain aneurysm. I made a couple of trips back East in the Lear, flying their family members, and bringing Gene home. Although we had been very close to Gene, this episode resulted in a much closer relationship with Gene's family, which still remains today.

After Betty passed, Gene began traveling a bit more. He went on several different trips with us, and also led us on our first trip to Israel. He also loved to hunt and fish, so we would fly to different places to do so.

On a trip Gene didn't attend, I took a group of Wichita businessmen to Alaska for salmon fishing. We took a float plane to an isolated fishing camp and were very successful in our catch. I took some salmon home, had it frozen, and was going to give it to Gene. I kept forgetting to take it to church with me. One Sunday evening Gene was preaching on how Christians should have fun and enjoy life. I quickly got up, drove home and got the frozen salmon out of my freezer. When I walked back into the church, Gene was

> *What can be said of the Christian leaders that have influenced me? John Henry, Joe Wright, Mark Royer, Brent Van Hook, Bishop Gerber. I want to thank them for their influence in my spiritual life.*

still preaching and saw me walking up the aisle. He started to shake his head no, but I walked up on the stage and plopped the frozen salmon on his speaker's note holder. It made a huge flop-sound, and the whole congregation broke up in laughter.

Over the years, several women tried to court Gene. Most of them we didn't approve of. He was a great guy, a man of God, and we could tell they were after him because he was a good catch, as opposed to really caring for or loving him. He did listen to our friendly advice.

Then one Sunday morning after church he asked Renae if she would stand up and hug him. When we asked why, he said a friend wanted him to meet a super woman who lived in Florida and gave him her height, so he wanted to see how that worked! We all laughed, and Renae graciously obliged.

It must have worked well, because after a few flights to Florida, they wound up husband and wife. Gene and his wife Joyce did a lot with us over the years. Gene retired from the church but started Shepherd's Fold Ministries. They minister to ministers. Gene died a few years back and is sorely missed. But his lovely and talented wife Joyce, lives on and remains one of our best friends. She now lives in Nashville and has provided some help with this book, as she has written several books herself. Joyce, Renae and I remain close friends today.

Joyce and Gene Williams

On our first anniversary, we had said we would go back to Hawaii where we celebrated our honeymoon. We didn't go back for five years. But when we did return, we bought a condo on Maui on a fluke, "You get a free dinner if you go look at a condo" deal.

Our friend Larry Steckline was with us and bought one at the same time. He didn't have ANY money on him, so I even had to pay his down payment for him. What a friend! In the three years we owned the condo we went there twice. I finally sold it to Larry's son, who I think, still owns it.

We had thought, since we were flying to Maui six times a week with the DC-10s - three times a week out of San Francisco and three out of Los Angeles with planes having 389 seats - we would go there more often.

What happened? We were paying so much attention to the business we only went there twice in the three years we owned the condo! Sometimes the things you want to do, you don't take the time to do. Laying on the beach in Maui sounds great, but when you're busy working, it doesn't happen.

Back to work...

The Seemingly Impossible

We had sixty days to make it happen!

The Indianapolis USPS Sort Center

In the meantime, Emery Air Freight received their three-year USPS contract to fly nine DC-9s and eight B-727s, basing them around the country, including Puerto Rico, flying in and out of a sort center the Postal Service had built in Indianapolis. Never having operated DC-9s, we had all the normal prep work to do, including proving runs; FAA approvals and the inevitable mountain of paperwork – and we only had 60 days to get the contract going. We were in good shape, but it quickly became apparent that the people at the new Emery Airlines weren't going to meet the time deadline. The current owner of the USPS contract, Del Smith of Evergreen Airlines, was intentionally setting roadblocks to frustrate our efforts.

We only had 30 days remaining when I called Emery's chairman and laid it out for him. I knew they wouldn't

make it in time, but if Emery would give us the 727s <u>that day</u>, we could make it happen. I knew these were, for the most part, the same planes and many of the same crews who once flew for us. It wasn't long before the chairman, Roger Curry, was on the line, saying those planes were now ours, and that he wished us luck.

We did make it happen. Through the combination of hard work by everybody, and a cooperative FAA office, we made it. It was one of those rare moments, that first night we flew into Indianapolis. Aircraft lights were like stars in the night sky, lined up to land, as far as our eyes could see.

According to the contract, Emery had control over the planes, and also the sort center.

The USPS only had one plane painted in their colors, so the ground controller tried to marshal it to its designated place. In the process, its wing struck a parking lot light pole situated quite close to the ramp. When the pilot deplaned, he was understandably distraught, believing he'd be fired. My

The Indianapolis Sort Center at Night

wife, Renae, was there and had witnessed all of it. She assured the pilot we knew it wasn't his fault. The rest of the night I marshalled the flights in myself, wearing my business suit, to avoid any further catastrophes. Investigating later, we found that same light pole had been clipped three previous times in the same way. That, however, was the airport's issue. We had bigger ones.

True to our reputation, our planes were always on time. But at the time, the mail was shipped in onionskin sacks. When unloading aircraft, crews were putting the sacks onto the conveyor, those sacks were snagging on the belts and getting chewed up, eventually breaking the expensive belts. What a disaster! I told both Emery and the Post Office people they all should have known better than to put sacks like that on a conveyor. Because of all the stops and starts to clear or fix the conveyor belts, all our planes were very late getting off the ground, and it was the same thing the next night.

The third night, Emery's big man himself, Chuck, hid in one of our planes. He'd instructed all of our air crews to take off on time, even if still empty. The USPS folks were upset, but Chuck had read the contract's fine print that required our aircraft to reach their destinations on time. It did not stipulate there had to be mail on board. Proving we could hold up our end, USPS started putting their sacked mail in cardboard boxes—and everything changed. Problem solved.

After a couple of nights of consistent on-time delivery, the top Post Office man told me it was obvious we knew what we were doing; and since the USPS had managed plenty of sort centers, they knew how to keep things humming on their end.

On the fourth night, every flight and its mail arrived on time, when who should call but the founder, owner and president of Evergreen Airlines, Del Smith? "So, you guys are really going to pull this off, huh?"

I retorted, "Of course we are!" He admitted he'd kept all his crews on standby and all planes ready, because he was sure we'd fail. In fact, he'd been helping us fail. That way, he could be the great white hope, sweeping in to rescue the faltering USPS and keep his contract as Evergreen had been flying most of the mail up to that time.

I think he knew getting that many planes flying in 60 days is nothing short of a miracle, especially considering all the purposeful interruptions he'd helped cause. We required all our "new" aircrews to complete our training, according to our high standards, regardless of their prior experience or what aircraft they'd been flying. We're talking ground school, flight simulators, and check flights in the airplane.

At the Indianapolis sort center, Emery had been parking their 727s tail-on, to their office area. The minute I saw that, I began telling them that sooner or later, jet blast would level those buildings. Deaf ears.

Sure enough, I was awakened one night by a call. The office of the Emery ops chief had collapsed. He wasn't in it at the time, or he'd have been crushed. It was amazing how fast those planes got repositioned!

USPS Boeing 727

Orion Airlines

In late November, we received a call at our office from Orion Airlines: "You guys want to buy our airline?" This was from the airline that had threatened to strike earlier, if Emery tried to give those planes to us to operate. Bear in mind, Orion still had a poor reputation with Emery because of their threats of union walkouts.

First, I called Orion back and asked them about their existing contract with Emery. They said they were pulling the plug on their business by the end of the year and needed somebody to buy all their assets, so they could get a tax rebate and recoup some of their purchase money. Just a few years earlier, their owner had paid over 300 million dollars for Orion Airlines and now wanted to recover some losses on his taxes. But, he had to close shop before the end of the year. In order to get the rebate, they needed an asset sale, and were required to shut down the airline by December 31st in order to qualify. He also asked that I not to tell Emery anything, until the deal was made.

One, I don't do business that way. Two, I had a good personal and working relationship with Emery's CEO, Chuck Zubarik. The next thing I did was call him and fill him in on as much as I knew. He said there was no way Orion could just shut off the lights and lock the doors.

I made my ear sore on the phone, but after a lot of discussion among the three of us, Orion agreed to sell me all their assets except a passenger Boeing 747 hangar queen they'd named the Jumbo Dumbo. By then it was 1 December, and we had to get twenty-two more 727s up and in operation in 30 days.

We weren't really sure what we faced. Emery had always expected contracted airlines flying for them to maintain a 96% minimum on-time requirement and Orion rarely met it. I told my team we were setting a 100% on-time requirement. In order to do this, we had to get things organized, everyone trained, and all aircraft operational.

What's one more impossible task, right? By this time, that almost seemed to be our standard operating procedure. With our whole team informed, a can-do attitude and a lot of pride, we got it done. We set up a war room and filled entire walls with Post-It notes! On them, we wrote every necessary task that needed to happen in the next 30 days! Our people would scan them, taking down the ones they felt they could accomplish. When those were done, we'd cross those off our master list. It was simple, but very effective.

At one point, we had over one hundred crew members in Wichita for training over Christmas Eve and Christmas Day without an open restaurant to feed them. We couldn't even find an open McDonald's. I called a hotel-owner friend. He graciously opened his kitchen and brought his folks in and fed everybody. I never asked, but I'm guessing his kitchen staff made some good money over those two days!

By 31 December, we had an additional twenty-two 727s in full operation. And our on-time average? 98%. And often the 100% we were shooting for became routine. I was proud of our people and pleased with our association with Emery. We continued flying for them until we sold the airline again for the second and final time in 2004.

It took guts and grit to get things done. By this time, we had been prepped for it!

> *We never had a marketing department. We had more people asking us to do business for them than what we had the ability to do, because of the quality of service we provided, and because we were the best at what we did.*

Green Energy Ventures

I have always been involved in green energy because I want us to preserve and protect our earth without hurting those who can least afford to pay the price.

What's the cost? The price often costs the neediest workers' jobs, but does not solve the problem. I believe that Agriboard, which we call "The Global Building System," is part of the solution, as we have modernized the ancient Egyptian approach to building.

Discovering Agriboard

In 1988, I flew my brother Larry back to Burlington to attend Grandmother Ryan's funeral. Coming back, the sky was clear, but Kansas farmers were burning off wheat stubble, obscuring the ground. We were in my plane, the King Air, so shooting an instrument approach into Wichita was no issue. I told Larry, though, that someday I hoped this type of pollution would be restricted.

Later, my friend Ed Sykes and I flew to Yakama to meet with some of Larry's friends. They had the idea of using rice straw to make a building material, as rice straw burning was starting to be banned. Although I thought the idea was a good one, I passed on investing, as I didn't feel they were far enough along in proving the concept.

Ron and Renae with a piece of an Agriboard panel

A few days after returning from Yakima, Ed Sykes called me saying he'd found a Texas company, Agriboard, operating from Electra, that was using wheat straw to make a wood and drywall substitute suitable for building construction. We did a little research, finding Agriboard was already partially funded by government-backed loans; and the mill, built by a Raytheon subsidiary was still working to smooth out the plant operations.

At the time, Agriboard was making a 3.5-inch thick, four-foot-wide board of compressed wheat straw. We could make it as long as one hundred feet before having to cut it. It was very strong and had excellent insulating qualities. The standard cut off length was either 8 or 9 feet long, but it could be cut to any length.

A four-foot by eight-foot piece of Agriboard's compressed wood, known in the trade as CAF board (compressed agricultural fiber), could be supported on the four corners, and 1,000 pounds laid in the middle. There would be almost no bowing, and after three days, it would be as flat as when first cut. You could apply a blowtorch flame to one side of a piece of CAF, and after ten minutes, the temperature on the reverse side wouldn't vary by more than three degrees. We were able to obtain a two and a half hour fire wall rating on the finished panels. We also got tornado shelter construction approval after firing a two by four board at the panel at over 100 mph.

To use this in construction, we would insert the CAF board inside several different-sized 'boxes' made of OSB (oriented strand board), on the sides. Pre-engineered lumber finished off the edges, with one end male and the other female so they could be easily fit together and fastened with a keyway, glue and screws.

We could erect a solid building in a few days that was well insulated, left no construction waste, was incredibly strong, and was bug and fireproof. The best part? The price was still comparable to inferior, conventionally built structures.

Trying to introduce a new building product into the industry was no easy task.

The Electra Mill Fire

Over the next few years, we put up over 300 structures using that concept. We were talking with big companies like Walmart and McDonald's to build stores for them, and business was ramping up. I hired outside engineers with fresh eyes to redesign a new mill we'd build somewhere in the Midwest.

I figured it was time I hired a top-drawer sales manager when my plant manager, Mike Husky, called me. There was a large grass fire burning two miles from our plant! Two power lines had been rubbing together in 60 mph winds, and enough insulation had worn or broken away that the wires had arced, sending molten material and sparks down into the dry prairie grass. Driven by the wind, the fire burned right through our property. This was not good. In addition to the plant, we had two large storage barns filled with wheat straw and finished product awaiting delivery.

Mike told me that about noon, the fire department ordered us to evacuate the property. Our people all escaped, but the plant, both barns, and even the railroad ties from the tracks were burned up. The fire was so superheated,

even the concrete floor had exploded! What had been polished concrete looked like loose gravel flooring.

The only thing that had survived that conflagration was an experimental 900 square foot quality house we'd built, just using 3.5 inch CAF board and steel studs. Four foot by eight foot CAF panels using cold rolled steel studs comprised the inside and outside walls and the roof. That was a bright light, shining through all the dark haze and soot of the fire's destruction. The metal door had blown open and the only damage was some soot and dirt that had blown in. Once swept out, you couldn't tell there had been a fire.

We had built two other CAF homes alongside that one, using different materials for studs. The CAF walls and roof survived but the studs burned. We knew then that Agriboard had not been utilizing the plant for the best product. We had been using SIP (structural insulated panels), and should have been building global homes or both. In hindsight, we should have just been building global homes with our original product; it would have served the world and ourselves much better.

When I came up with the idea, I had some CAF panels shipped to Wichita. Then I used a downtown Wichita metal shop to build a proper house. We'd found we could build the entire house out of CAF board, except the foundation. It took less than a day to build a house with all the walls, roof, windows and doors completed for less than $5 a square foot, excluding the foundation. The guy who owned the metal shop wanted to know if he could buy into the company. We declined his offer.

Agriboard Global Expansion

We used this idea in Sri Lanka, building 10 such homes in the devastated area left by the tsunami of 2004. We provided all materials, and Walmart shipped them for us. I was planning to go see the homes for myself, but was told that the Tamil Tiger rebel group might see me as a kidnapping target and I was advised to stay home, which I did.

We did the same thing in Haiti, following their earthquake. At least, we tried. We did our part; however, dealing with the open graft and corruption of the Haitian government was a real eye-opener. We got our ready-to-build homes into Haiti as promised. But it took almost a year to get them released from customs! Everyone at every level required a "fee" (read "bribe"), even though those homes were desperately needed by their own people. We finally had them delivered and built, but only after a lot of money changed very greedy hands. The good news is that all of those Agriboard homes still stand today, and some deeply grateful people live in them.

Reigniting Our Agriboard Enterprise

There are two types of people in the world- grateful and ungrateful. Knowing that was good for me. I invested right at 20 million dollars and 10 busy years getting our Electra plant where I wanted it. A few hours of wild fire deleted all that work. To say I was devastated is an understatement.

What little insurance, compared to the investment I had made, the insurance company tried to keep from me. They claimed that since I hadn't turned much of a profit (yet), it was a good thing the plant burned; so they shouldn't need to pay. That reasoning was not going to fly with me. It took me seven years of litigation to show the courts that nothing could have been further from the truth.

I lost my investment in the fire, and knew I was under-insured, yet figured if the insurance company cooperated, I'd get about eight million of that back. Knowing we needed to honor our outstanding Agriboard orders, I made an offer to the insurance company that I'd settle for seven million if they'd pay out immediately.

They refused, choosing instead to drag the entire thing out over another seven years in court. I consistently won each case, finally recouping about 8.5 million in the process.

After all this, I asked our attorney, "Why did they drag it out, knowing they would lose?"

He said, "To them it isn't losing. They knew the longer they kept your money tied up in court, the longer they'd have to use it, keeping the accrued interest for themselves.

That interest almost always brings them more than they ever pay to their own attorneys, and in claims."

I got it, though that didn't mean it was right. I could see that under usual circumstances, policyholders were financially forced to settle for less than they were rightly owed.

Several good orders had burned up in the Electra fire, and we needed to fill them. At that time, we planned to rebuild somewhere else and wanted to save our existing customers. We located a building in Vernon, Texas, about 20 miles from our original plant and set up a temporary operation to fill those orders. We had to buy a competitor's two-inch thick straw board, which meant we had to use two layers to equal the strength and measurements of our own Agriboard. Yes, it cost plenty. Yes, we lost money in the process. But we filled all those orders and we kept our good name and credit.

After we'd fulfilled our responsibilities, we closed the temporary plant about a year after the fire, not knowing at the time that the litigation would take so long to settle.

I made the decision, along with my wife, not to rebuild the Agriboard plant if it required me to put up all the money again. Reality had overridden my passion. Common sense and wisdom had, for once at least, prevailed. I had some health issues to deal with at the time. I believed then, as I still do, that our combined efforts over that decade had proven the concept to be viable.

Structures built from compressed agricultural fiber were both stronger and far more eco-friendly in terms of construction waste than those made using conventional wood products. This was no longer a start-up venture but a proven, profitable concept. I am still looking for one or more investors to build a plant in the United States.

Agriboard in India

Sometime during the process, I'd brought my brother, Larry, on board full-time as he had been involved from the start. During my health issues and convalescence, he oversaw Agriboard, keeping the concept and dream alive. That choice paid off.

Larry got a call from some Indian nationals, business people living in America, but whose business ties were in their home country. They'd done due diligence in vetting Agriboard, both company and concept, and wanted to build low-cost, high-quality homes in India.

We owned the necessary patents, and we'd proven how to make the whole idea work. So, we formed a license agreement with them. As of this writing, they are at least 90% done with Agriboard's first new mill in India. And, get this: they're not only making the CAF board; they're also developing whole towns using our method, including the entire infrastructure!

Going Green

The process we use to create Agriboard has a negative carbon footprint. We were able to offer tax credits for green energy construction, and several of our customers saved quite a bit by using our SIP panels in their construction projects. Politics, greed, famine, earthquakes, hurricanes, and high construction costs have had so many people living in slum conditions. One of my solutions? Agriboard offers people the opportunity for a quality, safe, well insulated, strong home; which is fireproof and even earthquake proof. These homes will last longer than us.

We also started a company called Tri-7, developing high-efficiency electric motors using magnets, which generated next-to-no-heat when running. That may not sound impressive unless you've accidentally laid your hand on a running electric motor, even a little one. The other startling factor about Tri-7 motors is that they are over ninety percent efficient!

Numerous Projects & Patents, Including Pro-Tec-It

Working with windmills, water generating projects and high efficiency motors that don't generate heat was a natural fit for my next business venture. Along with my brother Larry, I've been involved with three different companies to this end. During the next several years, I focused my energy here and still do. We have now obtained numerous patents which can help bring more green energy into an affordable mode and bring some of these things to reality. Our most recent patents are for a waterproofing liquid material called Pro-Tec-It. It can be sprayed, brushed or wiped on just about anything including cinder blocks and it is waterproof, fireproof and completely green.

Commitment Takes Tenacity, Grit and Patience.
I've had quite a few expensive lessons, yet the value of preserving the earth, and improving quality of life is priceless. That factory fire made things change quickly. So much invested and it was gone in one afternoon. That litigation with the insurance company took several court battles and eight years to resolve, yet I was thankful I had enough money to hold out and not give in to an unfair settlement. Some may not have been able to hang on. I see what happened as another opportunity to stand up for what I believe in, and I encourage you to do the same.

The Business and Pleasure of Aviation

From natural disasters and international capers, to flying through the fall out of 9/11 attacks, we kept flying, while managing to have a little fun around the world.

Front from left: Ron, Ray, Beth, Jeff. Second row: Renae, Mary, Jack. Back: Danny

All over the Map

We helped build some of the greatest air charter, freight and passenger businesses in our country.

The Morris Air Story

One day a man from Salt Lake City, David Needleman, called and asked if we could help him and his company get their own FAA Part 121 certificate. I said sure, since we'd helped others do the same. Jack McInteer, Jeff Crippen and I flew out to Salt Lake City to meet with Needleman and his company, Morris Air. It took no time at all to figure out their problem.

Unless you already hold an air carrier certificate, you cannot advertise yourself as an airline. The Department of Transportation flatly told them to either change their name or get an operating certificate. Morris Air was, in reality, a travel agency. In addition to booking trips, they also trained travel agents. Owner June Morris was an impressive, sharp lady, who told us her husband counseled her to hire the best students for herself, and use them to build up a good travel agency.

She did, and soon found herself chartering several large planes from both Continental Airlines and a charter airline, Sierra Pacific. They were keeping several planes – Boeing 737-300s – busy, full-time.

We did our normal startup thing, initially leasing three planes, B-737s, then adding two more after things got moving along well. We needed the usual FAA proving runs and all the expected approvals, and got those done in short order.

On one such proving run, we were flying to Anchorage when our captain noticed a large, strange looking "cloud" that our present course would eventually take us through.

He got permission from the center sector to divert and was soon told it was a volcanic eruption. They said one plane had foolishly flown through it and lost all its engines, badly damaging the aircraft. Fortunately, they glided to a lower altitude and restarted one of them, which let them land safely, though with substantial airframe and engine damage.

As we kept dotting 'I's" and crossing 'T's' for the FAA, we had the planes painted in Morris Air's colors, but with our name on the side in removable paint.

All in all, the people of Morris Air were extremely hard-working, smart, self-motivated, easy to work with, and dreaming of their own operation. Our initial contract called for one year, but after nine months using our manuals and books, they got the Salt Lake City FAA to issue them their own certificate. They called me, asking if they could buy us out early on our contract. I love to see people doing what they love and going after what they want, so of course, I said yes. They not only paid us a fair price but also paid us for the books and manuals we'd let them use. And in the airline business, there are plenty of those.

From the very first flight, Morris Air inundated the airline terminal.

The first day we began flying out of Salt Lake City, Morris Air was advertising like Southwest, which was the airline they were imitating. Why not pick the best example? We had three planes ready, but due to the great ads, we had so many people filling up the terminal wanting on our flights that the other airlines couldn't get their passengers through to their ticket counters! It only took a few days until those airlines, mainly Delta and TWA, moved their ticketing operations elsewhere.

About a year after Morris Air had their own 121 certificate, David Needleman called swearing me to secrecy.

He said the next day the announcement would hit the media: Southwest Airlines was buying them out for $133 million dollars! I quickly and humorously asked David if I could quickly renegotiate our contact. This was the first of two airlines for which we flew that was bought by Southwest.

David Needleman obviously knew his stuff, as he went on to start Jet Blue out of New York, and later on began another airline out of South America.

Morris Air and Southwest (photo by Richard Silagi GNU)

al aircraft within a few years' time.

This attracted the interest of Robert Priddy, who bought Gary out and was running the airline himself. Eventually, he sold the airline which was then moved to Phoenix. Priddy then started another airline, ValuJet, based in Florida. They quickly grew using Douglas DC-9 aircraft.

ValuJet

When I was heading up our FBO at what was then Wichita Mid-Continent Airport, a startup airline called Air Midwest was based right next to me. Gary Adamson was the sole owner. He began his business with twin-engine Cessna 400-series aircraft. Like most startups, Gary struggled financially. We often talked about our mutual concerns, most often regarding finances.

Gary was lobbying hard for the Essential Air Services Act (ESS) that was stalled somewhere in Congress. I doubt Gary could have survived much longer, but finally Congress approved the law which subsidized the flights Gary was taking. He was then able to get subsidies for each flight out of smaller cities who couldn't support air service on their own. It was called Essential Air Service or ESS. He quickly upsized his fleet to turboprop Merlin-engine aircraft, then built it up to where he was operating sever-

As often happens for various reasons, negative rumors spread throughout the industry about possible reasons for ValuJet's fast growth. I sent him a note that we were also operating DC-9s, and if he wanted, we would operate some of his, while he got caught up on flight and maintenance training.

After the ValuJet crash caused by the improper hauling of oxygen generators, the new president called me wanting to know if that offer to fly some aircraft on their behalf was still open since the FAA had shut down all their own flights pending the investigation's outcome.

We went down to their headquarters in Atlanta to meet with them. They asked if we could handle 19 of their DC-9 planes. We told them if our FAA folks would approve, sure we could.

When we asked our great FAA people about it, they went into conniptions. They said if we operated any of ValuJet's planes, we'd be the most thoroughly scrutinized airline on the planet, and they strongly recommended against it. We listened.

Air Tran

That wasn't the end of the story, however. ValuJet's people came to Wichita to evaluate buying our airline and using it to rebuild theirs. While still talking about it, they told us they'd made a deal with Air Tran out of Florida. The two entities took the name Air Tran, and built up a quality, large Atlanta-based airline.

In 2003, Air Tran called and asked if I would be willing to fly several planes on their behalf, since their DC-9s were range-limited and they wanted to fly to the West Coast.

We agreed and negotiated a contract for four aircraft; three planes plus a spare. We painted them in Air Tran's colors and, except for the emergency exit cards and our name on the nose wheel cover, they looked just like Air Tran's birds. At that time we were operating three 737 models: the B-200, B-300, and the B-800. We also were operating several Airbus A-320s.

Air Tran picked the A-320s, so we leased four of them. After a short time, these were the highest utilized A-320 airplanes in the world, averaging over 500 flight hours per month. We had a two-year contract, and their pilots' union had already approved this deal since they knew one day they would be flying these very routes that included Las Vegas, San Francisco, and Los Angeles. The 320s proved to be so reliable that Air Tran decided to put our spare on a run to Miami.

We found ourselves flying more flight hours per month in the A-320 than anyone else in the world, averaging over 500 hours each month per aircraft. Being kind of giddy, I guess, Air Tran decided to order 100 Airbuses. When Boeing heard about it, they said they were going to call in the $100 million dollar note that Air Tran still owed them for the DC-9s. Wisely, Air Tran switched and purchased 100 B-737s instead.

Doubtlessly, the B-737 inventory helped them later on, when Southwest bought out Air Tran. I don't think Southwest would have been so eager since the only plane they have ever flown is the Boeing 737.

Once Air Tran got FAA approval to operate their 737s, they asked if they could buy us out of our contract, since we still had a few months left. As fate – or, more likely, faith would have it, when we leased our four A-320s, the market was very soft, meaning we got a very good price. But the market had come back up in the meantime. Therefore, those planes' value had gone up considerably as well, and we made money on Air Trans' buyout – plus we released the A-320s at a nice profit. This deal turned out to be one of our most profitable short-term contracts. We had a lot of very satisfied customers and a lot of fun in the process.

Southwest

Southwest's founder, Herb Kelleher, got his start flying Cessna 400 series aircraft out of Love Field in Dallas, Texas. His flight attendants were all young, pretty girls who wore red tight short shorts and low-cut blouses. Back then, it did the job. One couldn't get away with that today.

Business travelers booked almost exclusively with Herb. He booked enough to go with larger aircraft. Herb picked the B-737, and Southwest has stuck exclusively with that type aircraft, though upgrading the fleet as different models became available. By utilizing the same model planes, their pilot and maintenance training costs were, and are, reduced substantially, along with many other cost and operating factors.

After Southwest had been in business a while, Dallas/Fort Worth International (DFW) was built and the cities of Dallas and Fort Worth established some restrictive rules that limited large aircraft and flights to cities outside of Texas bordering states. Herb, although I think he would deny this, was able to get Senator Jim Wright to have Congress pass what was called the Wright Amendment.

Technically, it backed this city restriction, but made an exception that you could operate a large aircraft out of Love Field providing the state you were flying to bordered Texas. A large aircraft was defined as having more than 56 seats. That law basically gave Southwest a monopoly operation out of that airport. When anyone flew Southwest out of Love Field, they would need to make a stop or change planes in a state that touched the borders of Texas. That law stayed in place for a lot of years even though it was challenged in court many times.

Herb Kelleher was a genius in starting, building and running a great airline, and keeping very high morale with his employees and unions. Unfortunately, Herb died recently and will be sorely missed. He was one of the great pioneers in aviation and his legacy lives on.

The Sky Service Story

A good customer or ours, Sky Service, was a large travel company based in Europe, for whom we flew the two DC-10s. They also had a new B-737-300 they wanted us to fly from Philadelphia to Las Vegas three times a week.

In Europe, airlines are charged a landing fee based on the published flight manuals gross weight. Because most of their trips over there are shorter, they opt to buy a flight manual with a lower published gross weight. Once we got the B-737-300 to the states, we discovered we could not fly it non-stop on this route, which presented a big problem.

I went to Boeing to see if I could get the flight manual with the higher weights since the plane was exactly the same with either manual. Boeing wanted $98,000 for the manual, stating that was the discount they gave Sky Service for getting the lighter weight manual. Both Sky Service and Ryan argued with Boeing about it, but in the meantime, we needed to make a fuel stop for these gambling junkets.

I decided we would land in Wichita. We could service and fuel the plane and, while the plane was on the ground, we'd conduct a raffle for money to be used at their destination casino.

At first, making a stop for our customer, Sky Service, was seen as negative, but after the first couple of trips,

If you aspire to travel, and don't have all of the resources you'd like, get a job with an airline or a travel agency.

most passengers loved the raffle. Remember: the planes were full of casino-bound, eager-to-gamble passengers.

We would take the seat number, put it into a hat and have someone draw. Often, we were fueled and ready to go before the passengers were done 'raffling'. A few weeks later, after we got the heavier weight manuals, we had customers whining because we weren't stopping to have the raffles any longer. Now, that is what I call a lemons-to-lemonade story!

Putting the DC-10s on our certificate was a real challenge. We'd been flying charter passenger planes for Sky Service USA, which was a wholly owned subsidiary of Sky Service of England. One fine day they asked if we'd be willing to fly a couple of DC-10s three times a week to Hawaii; one from San Francisco and one from Los Angeles. We said, "Sure."

They found the two planes and had them refurbished and repainted in England at a mere ten million dollars per plane, which didn't include the purchase price. Crazy, right?

Each one of them had 389 passenger seats installed, so I called them our cattle cars. If you've ever seen a DC-10 lumbering along a taxiway, loaded to the gills with people, that'll make sense.

Sky Service USA was late getting their first plane out of maintenance, so we subcontracted out that first season to Omni Air out of Tulsa, Oklahoma. Though our competitor, we respected them and they offered us first-class service – at a first-class price. We were in business.

We finally had both our DC-10s almost operational. However, our local FAA didn't know DC-10s. In our emergency evacuation demo, there was always one slide that, when deployed, wouldn't touch ground; it always ended up about a foot above the ground, and the FAA refused to approve it. Every such demo was costly in both time and dollars. So, we finally flew the plane to Kansas City and repeated the demo in a TWA hangar where the wind couldn't artificially hold the emergency slide up off the ground.

On some of the first few trips, our flight attendants complained the plane leaked and wasn't safe. We found that when those aircraft were being refurbished, the insulation behind the cabin panels hadn't been correctly installed. When at altitude, condensation was forming ice; then when descending, the ice was melting and dripping from above the windows. To be fair, it did look like a leak. So, until we could get the insulation properly redone, I rode in that plane for a week or so to prove flying in it was perfectly safe. Anyway, the crews, all appreciating my willingness to put

Interior of Ryan Aviation Passenger Plane

my backside where my mouth was, understood and were satisfied. Three or four trips to Hawaii. Stuck on a totally refurbished DC-10. Meals. Great service. But, hey—don't feel sorry for me. It's the price of ownership!

Speaking of which, on one of those trips back from Hawaii, I sat in one of the front window seats prior to passenger boarding for a little more leg room. These flights had no assigned seating, folks could sit wherever there was an open spot.

This one couple got on board, stopped in front of me, and the man said I was sitting in his seat! The flight attendant overheard him and immediately went to get the captain. I was polite. "Sir, these are charter flights, and have no assigned seating. I like where I'm sitting."

He developed a head of steam and started getting very belligerent when the captain stepped up and curtly told him to get off his plane because he was yelling at the owner of the airline, and we weren't going to fly him anywhere.

At that, the man became amazingly penitent. The wife never said anything to me, but after she led him to the back and told him where they were going to sit, I'm betting she said plenty to him. Probably not real nice.

A Note about Omni: After I sold the airline the second time, and Jeff Crippen had overseen Agriboard for a period of time, he took over as president of Omni Air and still remains there today. Unfortunately, Stan Burnstein, the founder of Omni Air and a good friend, died a couple years ago, but the airline still flies on. The airline just recently sold to another airline for over 750 million dollars, and Jeff has agreed to stay on for at least three years as CEO; I hope Jeff remembers me in his will.

Toucan Air

Another request to start another airline for another country. We were flying high!

Hong Kong was going Communist. Of all places, the little country of Belize on Central America's east coast contacted us, asking if we'd be willing to partner with them in starting up an international airline based there. Many very wealthy former citizens of Hong Kong were leaving and taking their money with them. They didn't trust anything the Communist leadership was promising them.

Since Belize was a former British colony, they felt they had an 'in' with the displaced people from Hong Kong.

They offered both citizenship and passports, if the newcomers would invest $50,000 USD in a new business.

At first, people were flocking to Belize, which fueled their desire to operate their own airline. We negotiated a contract, leasing a B-727-200 and having it painted in their desired colors, including a brilliantly-colored toucan on the tail, since the name of their airline would be Toucan Air.

On our maiden delivery flight into Toucan City, I was captain, and we had several high level government officials on board. We did several lows and slows overhead, showing off their colorful new passenger jet. Upon landing, there were firetrucks fountaining water while bands played. It was truly a big celebration, and we were treated like royalty.

I felt bad that Toucan Air flew a few trips, with almost empty seats. What Belize had found out is the Hong Kong transplants had decided Canada was a better place to relocate and begin their new lives. Regretfully, yet wisely, the good people of Belize abandoned the idea of their own airline, and Toucan Air was permanently grounded. However, the people were all gracious. They paid us what they'd promised and treated us well for trying so hard to help them.

Gold Transportation

We were contacted by Roy Goldberg, based in Atlantic City, who was running a very successful travel agency service. He wanted to set up an aircraft charter service where he would bring gamblers into Atlantic City from all over the country. We struck a deal, bought one B-737-200 with all coach class seating, and started flying for Gold Transportation.

We painted the plane a lot like the old Braniff Airlines colors which, you may recall, were very bright. Roy wanted his planes to stand out on the ramp, and did they ever! The one-plane operation turned into three planes. I bought one of those aircraft personally from Southwest Airlines, and used the plane in the Gold Transportation operation. After the plane had acquired over 80,000 hours, I retired it and gave it to the Kansas Aviation Museum, where it resides today.

Before we sold the second time, we were operating 60 large aircraft with 2500 employees and doing over 300 million a year in sales. The reason our airline was so successful is because we were very entrepreneurial-centered in how we put each of those deals together.

It was a lot more fun to be on the inbound gambling trip than the outbound one. During the Learjet charter days, it was common to get a late-night call from some oil guys, drinking, and wanting to go to Las Vegas. I learned quickly that on any of those trips you get paid in cash up front. We did a lot of them when oil prices were high and very few when they were low. Our crews were treated very well in Vegas, as most of the larger casinos knew we were flying in high rollers. Few left there with the same enthusiasm they had on arrival. Little did I know at that time, I would someday be flying in large groups of gamblers frequently on our own airline.

Roy wanted us to start up a separate airline based out of Atlantic City, of which he would be part owner. Roy was either too tight or we were too tough… and besides, I never wanted to sell tickets. We never were able to put a deal together but eventually Spirit Airlines saw the opportunity and did just that.

Competition and Friendship

Wholesale tour operators became some of our best clients. And some of our competing airlines became some of our best friends.

International Seasonal Service

When we started flying for the wholesale tour charter companies, and other charter companies, we were using older aircraft. It didn't make financial sense to use newer, more expensive aircraft, as the business was very cost competitive and seasonal. I came up with an idea to offset the costs. In Europe, most people take their vacations in the summer, while here they take them in the winter. The Department of Transportation did not allow foreign air carriers to operate out of the US, carrying passengers both ways. We talked with people we had met at Air Lingus, in Ireland, and found a way to lease their newer planes in the winter and give them back in the summer.

It was complicated and required that they adopt our training and maintenance programs or vice versa. We had to use our pilots and flight attendants, but made it work. We eventually started doing this with several other foreign carriers. Ray Thomas, by then our vice president of maintenance, figured out how to get the FAA and their

Apple Vacations using foreign aircraft

foreign counterparts to accept the way we were operating. The foreign airlines were losing money on the deal, but it was less money lost than just parking the planes. We were able to offer newer aircraft to the charter operators at a competitive price.

We made good friends with these airlines and remain good friends with several of them. We worked very closely with Pat O'Brian of Air Lingus, as well as many executives from other airlines. We were members of National Airlines Transport Association, NATA, as were most of our competition and scheduled airlines. I met and worked with top management of a lot of airlines in my career. I admit it was fun, being able to call up and have guys like Fred Smith of Federal Express and Herb Kelleher of Southwest Airlines, Bob Hoover, Clay Lacy, and Ross Fisher, to name a few, take my calls.

Miami Air

Ross Fisher started Miami Air, a charter airline, that we considered our strongest competitor. They started around the same time I did and continued to operate after I sold Ryan International Airlines. Whenever we had a plane break, we would try to use them, knowing it would cost more, but safety and reliability when trying to rescue a broken or missed flight is even more important.

The National Air Carriers Association, NACA, liked to have their meeting in Miami. Ross loved fishing and had a very nice fishing boat where he would take us deep sea fishing after our meetings. He would then have his yacht club prepare some of the fish for the evening meal. I am sad to say that during the coronavirus epidemic, Miami Air decided to cease flying and closed their business.

When I was ready to say goodbye, after I had sold the airline, the organization told me they weren't ready for me to go. I was pleased and proud they made me a lifetime honorary member of NACA.

Saving the Day

I had been on the road and was at a meeting in Las Vegas when Jack McInteer and Jeff Crippen asked how quickly I could get to San Francisco (SFO). Another airline had a serious mechanical problem and wanted us to fly their trip. Although by chance, we had a B-727-200 in SFO at the time, the cockpit crew was out of time. I flew the Lear to SFO, got on the plane full of passengers and radioed ATC for my clearance. We found, after some troubleshooting, one of the radios was stuck in transmit mode. Without having any of our maintenance people there, we elected to turn that radio off and proceed, which we did uneventfully, as we had two other radios. The flight was to Kansas City, then on to New York (LGA). A fresh crew met the plane in Kansas City (MCI). I went to bed. The plane went to LGA with the radios all working properly. Pilots are limited in the amount of time we can be awake, and in the amount of time we can fly. Proximity and precision saved the day.

A Fare Resolution

One day I received a call from a travel firm that handled Proctor and Gamble's travel needs. They were using Sabina Airlines and Delta Airlines to fly their executives between their US and Brussels headquarters. They couldn't get the terms they wanted, so they had threatened both airlines, telling them if they didn't comply, they would get their own plane.

We knew they were negotiating with the airlines, but in the meantime we agreed to fly an Airbus A-320 to Brussels three times a week. Using the A-320 required a fuel stop, so we suggested using a B-757, which could go non-stop. They didn't want to pay the extra costs and said a fuel stop would be fine.

We found an A-320, had it painted in the colors they wanted, and put in fifty plush first class seats in the cabin. The P&G people seemed to like the stop in Iceland; they'd buy souvenirs for their family, and they could stretch their legs while we refueled the plane. Sometimes the plane wasn't full, so we often had ride-alongs wanting to take the trip. Things went very well, and after eight months they called and said Delta had made them a deal they could not refuse. Can we buy you out of the months left on the contract? Once again, the plane we had leased had gone up in value, so we again won on both ends.

A Deal I Wouldn't Do

I was asked to go to Haiti and meet with a casino owner and his son to talk about starting airline service to the casino. It quickly became clear to me, this was a contract that I wanted no part of. After doing some background checks on the owners, I knew I might be in real trouble.

While trying to stay out of sight, a cab driver asked me if I had ever been to a Voodoo ceremony and would I like to go to one. I said sure, not knowing anything about Voodoo. He said he would pick me up at nine that night. He never showed up. I found out later that the casino owners heard about this and stopped the pick up as they knew I would have been an unwilling participant in the ceremony, probably never to return. Another angel. I told them I would get back to them on price and availability, but never did. I just wanted to get home safely.

Flyin' Fish

We operated three Boeing 727s for about five years, landing on old WWII runways in Saipan and Guam and all of the outlying islands we served.

Alaska Wind and Weather

One day a man named Mike Quinn came into my office announcing he wanted to start an airline based out of Guam, flying fresh tuna. He was an ex-military pilot who also wanted to fly our planes as a crew member while we helped him get his own FAA 121 certificate. Sounded doable.

We leased a B-727-100 cargo model, had it painted, and flew it to Guam. Simple, right? Well, you know by now very little is ever simple with me. That trip wound up being one of the few times in my flying career I seriously thought everyone on board, including myself might die before getting home again.

We flew to Anchorage, where we stopped for fuel. Then, after checking the weather, we took off at night for the Aleutian Island of Adak. When we passed our point of no return, we got Adak on the radio, and they told us their weather had worsened. They reported freezing rain, icy runways and winds over 70 miles per hour out of the southeast, with cloud ceiling at ILS minimums. Okay, that may be normal for Adak, Alaska, but it's nowhere near normal for Ron Ryan.

Adak's ILS approach was to the southwest, but with the winds and icy runway, our only alternative was to circle and land on the south runway. We had two captains on board plus myself, and I was in the jump seat right behind the command pilot. Renae and a pilot's fiancée, who was a flight attendant for another airline, were with us. We were fortunate to have a military pilot on the ground who talked to us, warning us not to stray from the centerline of Runway 18 South, because of the mountainous terrain, locally dubbed, "Stairway to Heaven." As if that wasn't enough, there was also a volcano about 22 miles to the northeast, it was pitch black outside, and snowing heavily.

While shooting the approach, the wind was so powerful that the captain let the localizer needle swing clear off the scale so that the ground radar controller, who could see our flight track on radar, told us to do a missed approach. Even with plenty of fuel, we really did not want to do that. We didn't have plenty of fuel. There was a severe pucker factor during that climb.

On our second attempt, even though the captain was crabbing 30 degrees into the wind, I could see the localizer needle steadily swinging off-center. The only thing worse than flying like that is having to watch someone else do it. I energetically hit the captain on the back, yelling, "TURN INTO THE NEEDLE! WE ARE INTO RESERVE FUEL!"

Fortunately, he listened. By the time the needle began to center, we were crabbing at almost forty-five degrees to the runway heading! We broke out of the clouds at about 400 feet above ground with decent visibility – but it was at night and the plane was at a 45 degree angle to the runway. We shot the ILS to runway 20, so we had to sidestep over to the South runway in the dark. The plane was relatively straight and aligned on Runway 18, but with the strong, gusting winds and icy surface conditions, it was one hairy, scary ride!

The minute all our wheels were on the ground, the captain used the thrust reversers, which immediately caused the plane to begin side-slipping, heading off the runway!

I'm not proud. I smacked the poor captain on the back again and yelled, "GET OFF THOSE REVERSERS!"

I think he was either too startled not to comply, or glad he could blame somebody else if things went south. Or east, or . . . wherever we would have been headed. As it was, when he retracted the thrust reversers, the plane steadied. With the strong winds on the nose, combined with the light load, we managed to stop quickly enough, although it sure felt like a long time.

You know that old joke, "S-L-O-W-L-Y I turned, step by step . . ." That's how we taxied, following the ground marshal's wands to the fueling ramp. Problem was, he didn't turn us, so our nose was into the wind. I told everybody to stay put, as the captain shut down the engines. Sure enough, the big 727 weathervaned around until facing into the wind. The fueler then chocked the wheels.

I climbed into my snowsuit, and after telling everyone to stay on the aircraft, went out to supervise the refueling. It would've been funny if it wasn't such a desperate situation, because the first guy who tried to hook up the fuel hose got blown off his feet, skidding across the ramp on the ice until he hit the security fence! How they got us refueled is yet another event in a long list of miracles in my life.

We'd been smart enough to prearrange fuel payment, so all I needed to do was go in and sign for it. The guy inside told me if the wind had been blowing any harder, they wouldn't have been able to get us fueled and off again. I wondered at the time if the wind could blow any harder, but the look in that guy's eyes pretty much said it all: "You have NO idea."

Photo of Welcome Sign in Alaska

When I got back aboard, the captains had switched seats, but I was still in the jump seat, right behind the command pilot. Once we had all three engines started, even before we released the brakes, the plane began sliding toward the fueling building.

I yelled, "USE THE REVERSERS!" The fresh captain informed me our FAA regs did not authorize our using thrust reversers to back up. I rather rudely and bluntly explained that the fuel building couldn't read those FAA "Part Whatever" regs, and if he DIDN'T use the reversers, the very least we'd do is cream the building. Fortunately, he knew wisdom when he heard it, and after engaging the thrust reversers, the unplanned forward motion stopped.

We found by selectively using the reversers, we could more or less guide the plane back into takeoff position. By this time, it was light outside, although the clouds were still a solid gray, and we still had to contend with 60 mph winds. Gingerly, we taxied/reversed out into position on Runway 18. As the captain had begun to line up on the centerline, I suggested getting on the upwind side of the runway. Even with a full load of fuel, we had a very short takeoff distance; but by the time we'd rotated, the plane was on the other side of the runway, as I'd thought would happen.

On to Guam

That night and morning experience on the Aleutian postage-stamp of Adak, Alaska, gave me a much greater awe and respect for the men and women who routinely fly in and out of that island chain. It's also likely the closest I ever came to meeting my Maker in an airplane.

Our next fuel stop was hot, sun-washed Wake Island. Talk about your study in contrasts! But we stopped there just long enough to refuel, then headed on to Guam.

Shortly after we began operations from there, Mike Quinn had us add another B-727 freighter. At first our flight crews weren't keen on being based out of Guam until they discovered world-class scuba-sea diving at some of the islands we served.

One night, we got a call from one of our captains based in Guam. He said he'd just witnessed a Korean 747 crash right in front of him, killing more than 300 on board. Our pilot said they'd just returned from a night trip, and Guam had some broken clouds. He and his crew elected to let the 747 shoot the approach first, while our flight went into a hold.

Our pilot said they all were thinking the giant Boeing seemed too low, when it suddenly burst into a huge ball of flames! Subsequent witnesses agreed, saying the 747 crew flew so low they almost clipped the VOR because they had used the wrong approach for the runway they'd been assigned.

My crew did seek out counseling. However, the whole thing disturbed them to the point they said nothing about thinking the plane was too low. Pilot etiquette and professional courtesy dictate that one captain rarely tells another he thinks he's doing something wrong. In this case, they all wish they had spoken up. Those kinds of things stick with a man.

Saipan International Airport
Ryan Apartments ↓ (½ Block off Beach)

WWII Runway in Saipan

Federated States of Micronesia

The Federated States of Micronesia wanted us to operate a plane for them. We leased a 727-200 heavy and had it painted as they wished.

Mike Quinn went his own way, still trying to get his own airline. He went so far as to hire a competitor of ours, Kitty Hawk, to fly a B-727, which he kept next to ours. Suddenly, we began having more than the usual mechanical problems. One day our mechanics said they were headed for lunch but stayed behind and observed the Kitty Hawk mechanics sneak over to our planes, steal parts they needed, then put their defective ones on our planes. Tom Christopher was the owner of Kitty Hawk and at one of our NATA meetings, I brought up this subject. He got mad at me and walked away only to come back later and apologize for the whole affair, claiming he did not authorize stealing parts off our plane. I think he called to see if I was telling him the truth. I can see how his people may have kept this from him.

The FBI was involved, but we never filed or pressed charges against Kitty Hawk. Their operation soon dried up, and they left the islands where we still had three planes in the air almost every day, with sometimes more than one trip per day. We could easily carry forty thousand pounds of fresh tuna per flight, and the Japanese were paying over $80 per pound by the time that fish was plated and hit their tables!

We did okay, flying out of there for about five years, until Mike Quinn finally convinced his investors to quit using us, and instead, use the airline he'd begun. It was only a year or so later that Mike ran his plane off the end of one island's runway, causing a bunch of damage to the aircraft and confirming our concerns about his piloting skills.

Federated States of Micronesia Plane

Continental/Micronesia was the only airline service for the entire area, and we'd maintained a good relationship with them. Our planes were based more on Saipan than on Guam and from there, we could go to the outer islands, all of which had at least five-thousand foot runways, built during World War II. We regularly flew in and out of Pohnpei, Chuck, Yap, Kosrae, Palau, and Rota. Also, we often made special trips to other islands to pick up fish.

Occasionally, we transported cars or heavy equipment too big for the belly cargo space on Continental/Micronesia's planes out to the islands. Bear in mind: these islands were very minute specks in a very large ocean. The only means of navigation they had were automatic direction finders (ADF), with weak signals even when turned on – which they weren't always. An early GPS system was in the works but hadn't yet been approved for navigation.

Where there's a will, right? The pilots only had handheld units that they would place up around the glare shield to try to get a good signal. I went to my FAA guy and asked permission to install a GPS antenna on each of our planes.

At first, they wouldn't budge. But after riding along with us a few times, they realized the danger and risk involved, and what they were asking of all fliers out there. They agreed to let us put in the antennas, which, they said, could only be used in an emergency and warned, that they

had better never hear of one of us getting lost while using one of those devices.

Okay, here's the deal. The primary radio communications were only HF, high frequency, which is notoriously unreliable, but they were required to get our flight clearances. I already mentioned the ADF system, and in that part of the world, cell phones weren't available. All of this adds up to aerial navigation and communications being difficult, to say the least.

We all agreed amongst ourselves that any flight over that vast expanse of ocean, trying to locate such a tiny target, constituted an emergency. And, further, we all agreed the FAA would never hear a peep about any of us getting lost while using our GPS units because we didn't plan on telling them in the off chance it ever did happen.

Tree Huts

Our company president at the time, Jeff Crippen, and I would fly out to Saipan and Guam at least once every six months. They came to know us, we befriended many of them, and they routinely treated us very well every time we were there. When we started the plane service for the Federated States of Micronesia, we flew it to Pohnpei where there was a band to meet us along with a lot of local and area government dignitaries who threw a grand party for us.

After the party, they took the flight crew to a hotel, but said they had a special place just for us. After being driven for about an hour, we passed some tree houses. You know me, right?

"Hey, Jeff—I think that one's your room!"

Our driver glanced into the rearview mirror and politely said, "Oh, no sir, Mr. Ryan. That one is yours."

We ended up staying in a resort featuring only tree houses, with only rope bridges connecting them! Now, Jeff is afraid of bugs. All bugs. Or snakes or – well, you get the picture. Our rooms were up pretty high in the trees, and when we got into our rooms there was mosquito netting over our beds.

Our guides had told us both once we got into bed to turn out the light, and pull the netting around us, because the windows only had screens on them. I could see that Jeff left his lights on all night. The next morning, he had so many little crawling friends on his net he had to holler for help just to get up!

A Close Call

Midwest Corporate Jet was doing maintenance on my King Air A-90. The plane is pressurized, and after a major inspection by MCJ, the cabin entry door leaked and made a loud squealing noise.

Jeff Spangler had been my pilot, who later went on to work for the FAA. He took the plane up for a test flight with a co-pilot, so he could go back to see if he could determine where the door was leaking. He was grateful for the fact that he had buckled the seat belt on the toilet seat right across from the door because while feeling around for the leak the door blew open!

The rapid depressurization threw the door open so hard it broke the door cables and wrapped the door around the belly of the plane, sucking the insulation out from behind the interior coverings! It scared both of them half to death, and especially the co-pilot, who was just sure Jeff had been sucked out of the plane. Jeff made his way back to the cockpit, declared an emergency, and landed safely. However, with the door hanging down, it dragged along the runway and created even more severe damage.

Enter Wendy Snow, the attorney who had introduced me to Jack McInteer. Wendy represented the insurance company that insured Midwest Corporate Jet. After an extensive investigation, we discovered MCJ had been grinding off the lock over cams that helped hold the door in place. This was not only stupid, but illegal.

Wendy kept arguing that while in the back, Jeff Spangler turned the door handle and caused it to open, therefore they wouldn't pay. My insurance paid up to the deductible amount. They also let me know how dishonest and deceitful a lawyer and insurance company can be. Because Wendy Snow had introduced me to Jack McInteer, I thought he couldn't be all bad. But Snow remains less than reputable. Other than that, perhaps he's a nice guy.

A few months later I got a call saying Yingling Aircraft had accidentally shut the big hangar doors and badly damaged one of the wings on the plane while working on my King Air. As fate would have it, the same insurance com-

From left: Ron Ryan, Jack McInteer and Jeff Crippen

98

pany that had lied and cheated on the door incident also insured Yingling.

The claims agent asked me what it would take to satisfy this claim and I told him, "Nothing short of a new plane!" After he almost had a heart attack, I told him flat out, I would not settle unless or until they paid my insurance company back for the door damage they lied about. He did agree to do that and after my insurance was reimbursed, they also paid to fix the wing damage, which was the least they should have done.

The Fayetteville Aircraft Paint Shop Fiasco

We'd done a couple of business deals with Robert Priddy prior to the whole ValuJet series of transactions; including buying the Air Midwest office building in Wichita to use as our corporate headquarters until we quickly grew out of that space. During that time, Air Midwest had leased an aircraft paint shop located in Fayetteville, Arkansas.

At the time I was still operating our FBO, and we had started doing more interior work on planes. So, we thought having our own paint shop might be the cat's jammies by way of enhancing the services we provided. At the same time, Robert Priddy had parked all his Merlin-powered aircraft and was preparing to paint them all, since they were still in the Air Midwest livery.

At some point, we'd signed a contract where I would paint aircraft from Air Midwest over the term of the lease. After we'd taken over, and only after much discussion, Priddy sent a single Merlin to be painted. While there, he then told me he wasn't going to paint any more of those planes, and that they were now my problem. Without a plane per month for a year, as was guaranteed in the contract, continuing to lease the paint shop made no sense. So, I walked away from it.

The city of Fayetteville sued Air Midwest, who promptly turned around and sued me. We went to trial in Fay-etteville, and the jury ruled Air Midwest liable, holding us harmless. At the time I was first considering the whole paint shop thing, I'd been talking with Clay Lacy of Lacy Aviation about being a partner. But after the hairy fur ball in dealing with Robert Priddy, I knew it wouldn't be fair to Clay. Later events proved me right.

I could write a book about what a colossal bad idea it is for an airline operator to own his own paint shop. But this one's challenging enough, so I'll just leave you with the Reader's Digest condensed version.

Don't.

Aircraft Adventures

There are so many things happening throughout the world, and flying is the only way to save time.

Twice the Speed of Sound to Switzerland

In the first airline, we owned an aircraft sales company. Doug Jackson, our lead salesman, found a Lear 24 for sale in Switzerland, and the price seemed right. Doug and I flew over, struck a deal to buy it, and told them we'd be back in a couple of weeks to take delivery.

On the return trip, we chose to fly the Super Sonic Transport (SST). I took my co-captain Mike Sweet, my attorney Jack McInteer and his wife Sandi. Settling back in my seat, I had no idea I was about to have yet another experience of a lifetime. The British Captain asked me if I'd like to join him as part of the flight crew that day! Seriously? Humbled and honored at the same time, of course I said yes. After checking my FAA license and medical certificate, the captain said I would be an official crew member. He also asked if there was a real emergency that I please go back to my seat.

The takeoff was a blast because they use afterburners until well airborne. The Brits referred to the afterburners as heaters. Once airborne, though, they are required to fly subsonic until out over the ocean because of noise abatement issues.

When we broke the sound barrier, the captain said to watch the pressure instruments like the altimeter and rate-of-climb indicator because they would fluctuate as the sound wave passes their exterior ports. Other than those indications, we never felt it when passing through the sound barrier.

We flew the remainder of the flight at twice the speed of sound, or Mach 2. Crewing the Super Sonic Transport was another highlight of my life!

Once on the ground, we took another, much slower plane to Zurich, where our new purchase was waiting for us. We had them do an engine run, checked the log books, paid them for the plane, and were set to head home.

Leaving the next morning, our first stop was Ireland, then Iceland, then Canada. While flying, we found if we advanced the throttles fast, it would produce a compressor stall. Experience had taught us this usually signals bent fan blades, and once on the ground in Wichita, we looked. Bingo! It only takes one, which is what we had.

Now the great price made sense. We took our new buy down to Strother Field, near Arkansas City and Winfield, Kansas, where GE has their CJ-610 engine repair shop. For not much cash, we got that blade fixed, and the engine purred like new. I offered to sell half-ownership of the plane to George Angle, KST&B Bank owner and CEO of Red Tiger Oil Company. I knew he could afford it. He had made a serious fortune buying a bunch of gold at market bottom and selling at the top. He just had to decide if he wanted it or not.

Nefarious Activities

In the meantime, C. Fred Shaw, a local and largest franchisee of Godfather's Pizza, also wanted to buy the plane outright, and did. Shortly after the ink was drying on that deal, George Angle called and said he'd decided he and his wife wanted to go ahead and buy half the plane. I had to tell him he'd waited too long, and the plane was already sold.

Fred Shaw based his new purchase with us and was all set with a pilot who used to fly for Elvis Presley. The pilot was also a skydiver, and shortly after his boss bought the plane, the pilot had an accident, and broke his leg.

Fred asked me if I could loan him a pilot until his man was hale and hearty again. As it happens, I did have a new hire from Flight Safety named Warren Smith that I could make available. He'd been flying for me for a fairly short time and was rated and typed in the Lear. Warren agreed to fly for Fred, but it wasn't long before he was concocting lies about the plane and our maintaining of it. It caught us by surprise. We couldn't understand it, and I made it clear we would do no more work on his plane. He tossed that off, saying he was getting his maintenance done elsewhere, although he kept parking the plane at our facility.

Everything about this was odd. When flying, Fred and Warren wore big, blingy gold chains. He looked nothing like a professional Lear captain, although he did resemble some other 'professionals' I'd seen. He showed up one day and told me Fred had offered him a flying job at a considerably higher salary. I told him I thought he was pretty low for pulling that when we were helping Fred out of a temporary tight spot.

I confronted Fred with everything. He said Warren had come to him, asking to be hired, and telling him I'd been paying him more than I actually was – another bald-faced lie. It was clear to me he was jockeying for Fred to offer him substantially more. Fred was either gullible or distracted, because he didn't get that Warren really took advantage of him. Though we allowed Fred to keep his Lear with us, I refused to have anything more to do with Warren Smith.

As it turned out, my instincts were right. One day Fred called, asking if I could disable his plane so no one could fly it without his written permission. Thinking he might be going through some domestic issues, we disconnected the battery and removed the current limiter.

Sure enough, at about 3 am the next morning, Warren Smith called our line service, asking them to get the plane out and fueled. When told the plane was disabled on the owner's orders, he abruptly hung up.

On our way out to the airport the next morning, we heard on the radio that a Lear 35 belonging to The Big Bend Coal Company had been stolen right from the factory. I put two and two together, and the minute we got to my office, I called a friend with the FBI and told him about Fred's and Warren's activities. He thanked me and said I'd just corroborated what they'd already figured, which was that Warren had stolen the plane while its crew was inside the factory filing their flight plan.

Warren had waited until the Lear crew got inside, then told the outside fuelers to top off the tanks. They'd no sooner complied than he got in, buttoned it up, started the engines, taxied out and took the active runway – all without a word to approach, ground control, or the tower.

I had suspected Warren's wife was mixed up in it. She'd told the FBI several things I knew were lies. We later found out Warren had been using drugs and also flying them in Fred's Lear. He definitely had gotten into the big leagues! It turns out he hadn't been keeping up with any maintenance on Fred's plane, but was paper-whipping phony repair bills and then getting AIFAM, the name of his company, to pay them. You're likely ahead of me again, but just in case, read that company name backwards.

Not the sharpest crayon in the box, right?

Among the many dumb things he did, Warren bought and registered in his own name both a helicopter and a fixed-wing plane, purchased with stolen money. He managed to duck any trouble for a time by spreading the rumor to Fred's controller that Fred was cheating on his wife; and since his wife worked in the office, the controller needed to just pay the bills quietly.

An FBI friend told me in all likelihood, somebody would soon find Warren's body because he was now on the run from the police – which meant he was of no more use to the drug traffickers. He had no one left to shill, or to protect him.

Though there was some brief communication with him after he'd stolen the Lear and taken off, no one has heard anything from Warren Smith since then, and the plane was never recovered. As far as we know, AIFAM went out of business, too. Maybe somebody told them the name was a little too simple, while a lot of people reading it, weren't. Anybody seen Warren Smith?

9/11 Changed Everything

I was on a travel agents' promotional trip being put on by Apple Vacations in Chicago. Afterward, I had flown to Milwaukee to attend the convention. Early in the morning, on September 11, 2001, Jeff Crippen called my room and said a plane had crashed into the World Trade Center! Several of our clients were headquartered there and I had been there many times. I was shocked.

I turned on the TV and was trying to figure out what kind of plane had hit the building on such a clear day. I could tell from the outside damage it was a big plane. I assumed that a fly-by-wire plane like an Airbus with redundant electronic controls had somehow lost them all and hit the building. While watching, I saw the second plane crash into the other tower! I knew then, this was no accident.

All aircraft were grounded. The FAA had enacted SCATANA – Security Control of Air Traffic and Navigational Aids. Though it was modified in that the US military left airspace control in the FAA's hands; and navigational aids and airport lighting remained operational to help airborne aircraft land swiftly, the FAA was nevertheless saying we had to get all our airplanes on the ground or they were in danger of being shot down.

Great. Just great. We had 33 planes in the sky at that time.

My wife Renae was the only person in management at Wichita. Renae told the FAA she needed me back in Wichita, said I was in the Lear in Milwaukee, and urged them to let me fly home. By this time Jeff Crippen and the others had rented a car and were driving back to Wichita.

The Kansas City Regional FAA Center told Renae they would give me a special code to fly as long as only my co-pilot and I were on board. They gave me a set of numbers. I went out, gave the code, and got my clearance to fly. Everyone at the FBO was stunned to see us get to take off.

It was eerie, as we were the only airplane in the sky except for some military planes. Not only did they use a different frequency than civilian aircraft; they did not look friendly!

Every time I was handed off, each controller would ask what my intentions were, and once I gave them my code, they would clear me into their airspace. It was about an hour and a half home, but it seemed like forever. We did manage to get all our planes on the ground, but they were scattered all over the country, with some even in Canada.

Many lives were lost and destroyed during the terrorist attack on the World Trade Center. It was one of those rare events in history that changed the fabric of the way the airline industry operated.

Flying the bin Laden Family

We had done a lot of flying for the government over the years, so the State Department was familiar with our operations. Way back, a DC-8 operated by a low quality and cost competitor had crashed, carrying a load of soldiers, and killing all aboard. We were called and asked if we would fly the honor guard to the crash site. We were told our costs were somewhat higher than the competition, but they wanted the best. That was quite an honor and the trip went off well.

On September 12th, I received a call from the State Department asking if we would be willing to fly the bin Laden family to Paris. I told them yes. We flew a B-727 from Miami to Los Angeles and picked up some of them; then flew back to Miami, where we picked up a lot more. The passenger manifest showed most of their names as "bin Laden kin."

The captain in Miami called me saying the flight attendants had figured out who we were flying and wanted extra pay to take the trip. I told him anyone who was scared did not need to go. However, I knew everybody was on edge, so we agreed to double their pay for this trip.

We flew from Miami to Baltimore, from where two of the planes had been hijacked, and picked up more bin Laden passengers on the way to Canada for refueling and a required crew change. Throughout all of this, we had more FBI, Customs, ATF and other government agencies than we'd ever seen in one place, thoroughly checking out our passengers.

Once we landed in Canada and the flight attendants got off, we fired all of them. If they had been scared and refused to fly, that would have been a separate issue; but to fly for more money was in my opinion, blackmail. We had a policy that if anyone got fired, they could appeal the firing all the way up to me, if necessary. Since I was the one who said to fire them, they came to me with their appeal. I found out from them what had happened.

An FBI agent had asked one of the flight attendants if they knew who they were flying. When she said no, he told her, "You've got the bin Laden family on board, and you should ask for more money!" Based on that fact, I brought all of them back except one who had been a previous troublemaker. I reported this to the State Department and that agent was fired over the incident.

Ramifications

Once again, we were flying when most planes were grounded and not hearing anyone on the radio is eerie. Sometime later that idiot movie maker Michael Moore stated that the flight was a stupid move, and that these people were probably guilty or involved in the 9/11 hijackings. Nothing could be further than the truth. They were totally vetted by many agencies, probably much better than that bonehead FBI agent. I was told once the American public knew it was bin Laden behind the attack, these people's lives would be in danger. Osama bin Laden hated his family for being in the US, and now the US would hate them just for being related to bin Laden!

Search Snopes.com

Fact Checks · September 11th

Did Saudis Fly Out of the U.S. While Airspace Was Still Closed after 9/11?

Rumor holds that a secret flight whisked prominent Saudis and Osama bin Laden's relatives out of the USA during a ban on air travel.

DAVID MIKKELSON
PUBLISHED 31 MARCH 2002

Snopes report about the evacuation of Bin Laden family members
(https://www.snopes.com/fact-check/flights-of-fancy/)

The aftermath of those terrorist attacks was astonishing. Of course, Michael Moore, being undisturbed by pesky things such as facts and the truth, made a movie about 9/11 with sickening, biased views that are just as putrid now as they were then. After 9/11, we were concerned we could go bankrupt, as we were unable to fly our regular runs.

As fate would have it, one of our biggest competitors went bankrupt first, and we were asked to pick up their flights, which was a lot more than we had lost. In their effort to keep the airlines afloat, the federal government put up 50 billion dollars for who could prove their losses during this crisis.

Because all of our contracts were cost plus, our customers were the ones taking the big hits, and the government's plan did not allow us to pass through the funds. When we only applied for a couple of million, we were repeatedly asked if we were sure that was enough. Some airlines asked for a lot more than they had coming; then during the inevitable audit, they were told they had to pay it back. But the government had not set up a system to do that, so the airlines kept the overpayment. Way to go, efficient government politicians! And how dare the airlines act like the government in keeping money that was not theirs?

As the saying goes, character isn't formed during a crisis; it is only revealed.

The Lear 35A

Having our FBO located in Wichita and owning an aircraft sales company often offered unique opportunities. I got a call from Rowan Drilling in Alaska. They had bought a new Lear 35A that they were having built at the factory in Wichita. It was one day before the delivery date, and though they had made a large down payment on the plane; they were short on cash.

At that time, the values of these planes were increasing because the demand was high. The prospective buyers told me they did not want the plane and would sell it to me for just what they had agreed to pay, which was 3.5 million dollars. Lear would not give them an extension.

Lear knew if the buyer didn't take the plane, they – Lear – could keep the deposit money, then turn around and sell that spanking new Lear 35A to another customer for an even higher price.

I happened to be out of town when I got the call, but told Rowen Drilling I'd try to raise the money by the next day, and if I could, I would buy the plane. I called my friend and then-banker, JV Lentell. At the time, he was president of The Kansas State Bank and Trust a bank owned by George Angle. I explained the situation and told him I needed 3.5 million for a Lear 35A, but needed it the next day and I was out of town. JV agreed to advance the money to me, and we closed on the plane the next day. I took delivery of the gorgeous plane and immediately put it up for sale.

I got a call from a guy in New York City who wanted to take a test ride in the plane. I flew to New York, took him on a two-leg trip, and returned to NYC that night. I had been able to mark the plane up $250,000 which was equal to new-plane pricing at that time. Yeah. That's how fast Lear's were appreciating at that time.

He agreed to buy and asked if I'd be willing to take his Merlin 3B in trade. It was a beautiful plane that had been featured on the cover of Flying Magazine just a couple months prior. I agreed. We flew the Merlin back to Wichita and put it on the market.

In hindsight, I made a great deal on the Lear but a lousy deal on the Merlin. No one seemed to want that airplane. One day we got a call from airport security saying there was a tornado sighted on the south side of the airport and we'd better get our planes protected.

From my FBO, I had an upstairs office balcony and saw one of my linemen towing the Merlin. I yelled down and asked where he was taking the plane. He said, "To the hangar." I yelled back and told him there would be big bonus if he towed it to the south side of the field.

We all survived that scare. Later that year, we did take a fun trip to the National Business Aircraft Association's meeting, where I finally found a buyer – although I gave up all the profits I had made on the Lear deal.

Alaskan Halibut

A side benefit is Rowland Drilling invited several guests and me to come up to Alaska and go fishing on their 50-foot Hatteras boat. I took my attorney, Jack McInteer, my Vice President Jeff Crippen, and Doug Jackson who headed up our aircraft sales department. Hey, I know who's important.

We flew up to Alaska, where we were met by some people who took us to one of their Twin Otters to fly up to Prudhoe Bay, where the boat was based. We took off and after a short time started to go through a mountain pass, because clouds obscured our visibility. Wisely, our pilot turned back and had a large helicopter pick us up. They'd obviously done this before, and flying through the pass that way was a lot safer.

We spent four days on the boat and caught a lot of fish, but the most fun for me was at night, bottom fishing. The depth was about 200 feet, so it took a long time to reel in anything we caught. I hooked a monster halibut as another boat pulled up beside us to watch.

I put in some real sweat equity, and took what seemed like forever just to get the thing to the surface. One of the guys on the other boat decided they would gaff the fish and help us get it on board. Unfortunately, when he swung his gaff, he hit my line and broke it!

Our boat's captain said my fish was well over a hundred pounds and had his pistol out to shoot it before we brought it on board. I really thought our captain was going to shoot the idiot who broke my line. Obviously, that boat disappeared into the mist.

I got back at it and soon hooked another eighty-pound halibut which we did get on board. The next morning, the cook made one of the best fresh fish breakfasts I had ever eaten. There are few blessings under God's Heaven like fresh-caught fish, prepared by somebody who knows their stuff.

My guys had all put scopolamine seasickness patches on before getting on the boat and left them on until after we got off. I have never been susceptible to motion sickness, so I didn't use them. The funny part, is they worked well while they were on the boat, but the guys took them off too early after getting off the boat and got seriously sick. It was called land sickness, caused by removing the patches too quickly once ashore. Don't take your patches off too early!

Ron Ryan deep sea fishing

105

Reflections

Don't let health problems
stop your life. It starts
in your head, and then,
listening to your wife…

A Heart Attack and Cancer!

While building our lake house out of Agriboard at Grand Lake, Oklahoma, something completely unexpected happened…

Let Me Drive Us

As is often the case, when an emergent situation has passed, its true cost becomes apparent. The accumulated stress of my non-stop life caught up with me, and I suffered a life-threatening heart attack.

Some time back, when I owned the airline the second time, we were returning from a motorcycle trip, with Renae on the back of my Honda Goldwing. Renae asked if I would pull over as we were passing the hospital. I wouldn't do it. My wife told me for two days that I was having a heart attack and I didn't believe her. My arm hurt and finally I said, "Honey, I think you were right, could you take me to the hospital?"

I had been in denial.

Not me, I get a physical every six months. I'm in great shape. I just have indigestion. I drank a whole bottle of Pepto Bismol and jumped on the trampoline to prove it wasn't my heart. After that manly display of "control" I said, "Honey, come on, let ME drive US to the hospital." And I did…

For me, the hardest part wasn't the heart attack, eating the humble pie was. It couldn't be happening to me.

It was necessary to fly me from Grand Lake, back to Wichita, where two stents were placed in my heart. My doctor was also a personal friend. The first thing he asked was why I was there and not at the club. I told him, "Renae told me yesterday, I was having a heart attack."

He responded, "I would not normally say this to a patient, but you're my friend. You're having a serious heart attack, and if there is something you need to do, or say to your wife, you better say it." He added, "I will step out of the room and give you some personal time."

I told her that I was alright with my God, and I was at peace if I died. We didn't have anything we needed to iron out because we kept our promise to our pastor when we married that we would not harbor anger, so Renae and I were also at peace with each other.

The month before my heart attack, Renae's sister-in-law Karen had passed of an aneurysm at 34 years old. She and Kelly, Renae's brother, had two precious little kids. Karen, who was a teacher, collapsed at school. So our emotions were very raw, as we were so concerned about her brother and our niece and nephew… Renae and her sister Cindy still talk about Kelly coming down the hall following Ron's surgery - all he said was "It's Okay." meaning it's okay that my spouse died and yours didn't.

I didn't want to be down in time. I wanted to walk out of the hospital and fly the next day. I was fidgety and Renae lay beside me to calm me down. We almost gave the male nurse who walked into my room a heart attack. He didn't know what to make of us! It took me about a year to get back to flying.

I'm aware coronary patients like me used to just die; I'm grateful for the advances in medical research producing those little wonders that saved my life. In July 2020, I had to have my aortic valve replaced in my heart. Once again, I was very impressed with the advances in medicine that allow for such miraculous surgeries. So far, so good!

Prostate Cancer

Because I took a flight physical every year, I knew my PSA numbers were increasing; so I went in to get a biopsy of my prostate. On Halloween of 2012, I got a call that I had stage 4 prostate cancer. I remember because we had just moved back to Wichita with our granddaughter and were preparing for her first big Halloween party. Kelly and Cindy came to our aid again, driving down and just sitting with us.

Obviously, we were quite concerned, and we needed to decide what kind of treatment or operation I should have. Once both sides of our family found out, we were showered with support and prayers. Renae and I went to several different doctors to research what if anything, I should do. I was pleasantly surprised, and pleased with the doctors. They spent a lot of time with us, explaining the options, risks and benefits. After much research and discussion, we decided to try CyberKnife treatments. There is no knife involved; but a series of concentrated radiation treatments, using gold rods (needles), inserted directly into the prostate. The five treatments were painless, although the side effects created fatigue; I slept for 12 hours following each treatment.

It worked! No lasting side effects and my PSA scores are great. As luck would have it at that time there were only five CyberKnife locations in the United States, and one of them was in Wichita. Anyone who has this kind of cancer, I can't recommend this procedure highly enough. I often think about how lucky I was, surviving a heart attack then overcoming cancer. Apparently, the Good Lord wasn't done with me yet…

Listen to Your Body

As men, we aren't typically as in tune with our bodies… I can hear a plane engine from three miles away and can usually tell you what type of aircraft it is, yet, I couldn't tell you that I was having a heart attack. It was because I've learned, from years of experience to listen to the engines, and later in life, to listen to my body.

Start practicing now, at whatever age. Your body changes every day and we're all growing older whether we like it or not.

It's critical to fine tune an airplane and to service and maintain it in good mechanical condition. Our bodies are no different, and you have to maintain them in good physical and mental health.

Looking back, I better understand the term "denial." I had heard that term before but hadn't really had the experience. I think Renae would have felt guilty if I hadn't listened to her, or that she hadn't pushed harder, had I not made it. I'm grateful that I'm alive and that I'm married to Renae… I'm glad that she saved my life.

Ron and Renae Ryan

Planes, Boats, Motorcycles and Aircraft Carriers

Looking back, it sure seems that any time a Lear was in the picture, I always had some kind of adventure, with a few of them not what I would have preferred. This one, however, was one of the great kind.

Mexico City

George Ablah had a friend, Dale Scuddy, who was both a used car salesman and owned Penn Yan Boat Company in New York. George must've told him about me, because Dale called and asked if I'd evaluate an older Lear 24 he owned. He even had it flown to Wichita, which was a nice touch. I mean, everyone knows I hate flying.

I gave it a good once-over and found it past-due for several major required inspections. I told him it would be more cost-effective to part the plane out, as it would cost him more to bring it up to FAA specs than the jet was worth. The plane languished at our shop for almost a month, when Dale called. He had a Mexican senator willing to buy the plane as-is, if I'd be willing to fly it to Mexico City. I would, and I did.

Night had fallen when we landed, and the tower directed us to taxi to a private hangar. Quite unusual. A man met and greeted us as we deplaned who said he represented customs, as well as the buyer. He mentioned that the senator bought the plane for his wife to go shopping in other cities. He then stamped our passports and took us to the terminal to catch our

Grand Lake Boat

flight home. Somebody had some pull!

Dale called after we'd returned, asking what he owed me. I'd thought about it, and said, "Nothing other than my out-of-pocket expenses." I figured that was that. It wasn't.

A Grand Gift and Grand Lake

Not too long after that, I was in my office attending to boring stuff when a man walked in and asked where I wanted the boat.

"Wha---what boat?"

"I've got a new, thirty-foot inboard Penn Yan boat outside for you. If you'll just sign here."

Seriously? Dale Scuddy had sent me a new boat as his way of thanking me for helping him sell that gray-haired Lear.

After getting the boat from Dale, I asked a Citation salesman friend, Don Love, if he'd help me get the boat to the Lake of the Ozarks. Back when I lived in Iowa, we used to go there.

Don did me one better. He said he had an open slip at his dock at Grand Lake in northeastern Oklahoma, and he'd pull my boat down there. He said if I decided I didn't like it there, he'd tow it over to Lake of the Ozarks. I was not familiar with Grand Lake at the time, but took him up on his offer. I thanked Dale for the boat, but only hung onto it for a couple of years before selling it for a better model. I sold everything at Grand Lake when we were setting up the airline to go public at Jack

McInteer's request; but once I sold the airline, I bought another residence at the lake. Thanks to Don's introduction, I've been at Grand Lake ever since, over 40 years, and absolutely love it. These are some of the highlights…

One day after repurchasing the airline, I got a pamphlet stating there was going to be a real estate auction, selling several condo units at Grand Lake. The time of the sale was about the same time I read the flyer! Renae and I looked at each other, then jumped into the King Air for a 45 minute flight, and went trampling off to the auction that was already underway. The Lear would have taken 20 minutes. Don't ask the difference in the cost.

When we arrived they were selling units at Island Park, so Renae ran through a couple of units, bid on one, and we got it. We used it as a summer home for a couple of years, then moved to a development on the golf course called the Chateaus. We were right next to Larry Steckline, known as the agricultural voice of the Kansas farmer. Larry was also a pilot and had just purchased a new Beech Baron. We flew together to the Lake on the inaugural flight. On landing, Renae opened a bottle of champagne and the cork almost took my head off! We still joke about that.

We lived in the Chateaus, until we built our Agriboard home, which we still have and love, over by the Cherokee Yacht Club, (CYC). It sounds too good to be true, but that Agriboard home is still like a new home.

CYC was owned by Terry Frost, who owned a bunch of 7-11 stores around the country. Years ago, he sold them all and did very well. Terry also lived by CYC, and was our neighbor. At one time, he owned a Falcon 10 jet, as well as a 125 foot yacht. When Terry and his wife Janet bought their yacht, he had it extensively redone in Florida.

Monaco

Terry was invited to have his boat in Monaco for a fund raiser to promote protecting the world's oceans; he invited Renae and me along and, of course, we accepted.

Terry put his yacht on a ship designed to carry yachts like his. We met the boat in Italy, along with Terry's new captain. We had planned on staying on the boat, but spent the first several days in Monaco in a very expensive, nice hotel. The boat had apparently been struck by lightning on the way over; and there were many electrical problems and failures.

After they got Terry's boat fixed, we moved onto it. There were yachts of all sizes and shapes, every one of them expensive. We went to several different ports, and along the way we discovered that the captain Terry had hired was awful, as well as dangerous. Terry fired the captain as soon as we left Monaco, and put the yacht back on the ship that would return it to Florida.

One night at a party, Renae danced with the Prince of Monaco. He was single, and the story was unless he married, he could lose his kingdom to France because the treaty required him to be married by a certain date. He married, since Monaco is still a separate monarchy. I couldn't believe how expensive everything was, but we had a great time.

The Falcon 10

I wound up buying half of Terry's Falcon 10 while we were living at the lake. I later bought out Terry's half and moved the plane to Wichita. I eventually sold the plane to an oil guy who lives in Newton, and he sold it and got into a time share deal. We remain good friends with Terry and his lovely wife Janet. I enjoy kidding Terry and often tell him, "Now that you've sold your boat and plane, it must be harder to find friends!"

Motorcycling

Terry, his wife Janet, Renae and I, along with several other couples at the lake often took long and short motorcycle trips. Frequently, we would have our bikes trailered to a city, then fly there and pick them up. We took many rides, and only once did we have a serious accident.

Art Couch from Tulsa hit a patch of sand in the mountains in Colorado. The bike they were riding went off the highway, through the grass, and into a ditch, throwing him and his wife off the bike. Art was right behind me.

I hit the same patch of sand, which almost got me, but I recovered, and he didn't. We took Art to the hospital for a bad gash in his ankle. Art recovered and started riding with us again, but his wife said she was done.

The Rescue

On one trip through the Smokey Mountains, we made a sightseeing stop on the side of the road. A couple stopped their car by us and said another car had just gone over the side of the mountain, just down the road. We drove down and sure enough, saw a car upside-down, way down the hill, with a woman hanging out the side window. We had to try to rescue them.

It was tough getting to the car, but our motorcycle boots helped. The husband was still trapped upside-down, in the car. We were able to cut his seat belt and get him out, but we were on the side of a very steep hill. Finally, the fire department and police arrived with long ropes. This allowed us to get the wife up the hill, and lower

The "Motorcyle Gang" in full Regalia

a stretcher for the husband. They were both taken to the hospital, and I assumed they both recovered.

We had motorcycle jackets with a lot of glitz and bling on the back (for the girls) and "studly" patches and rhinestones for us guys, reading "RUBs." So, when the local newspaper reported the story they named us Rich Urban Bikers; I changed it to Rural Urban Bikers.

We took a 10-day motorcycle trip through Canada with five other couples. We started in central Canada, rode to the West coast, stayed a few days, and rode back. We stayed one night at Banff to visit Lake Louise, both are just

as pretty as the ads and movie clips portray. We had a great time and saw some spectacular country.

On the return trip, we went through Omaha, where the chief of police for the motorcycle unit was Terry Frost's good friend; his wife was Terry's accountant. While we were loading up the bikes, Renae got a call and I saw her drop to the ground in tears. Her best friend, Wahleeta Steckline, had just been killed in a farming accident. We hurried back to Wichita to be there for, and console her husband Larry, our good friend. It was a sad time in our lives.

As time passed, we took Larry to a lot of places and wound up buying a condo together in Naples, Florida. After a couple of years, Larry married Carla Stovall, who at the time was attorney general for the State of Kansas, and a shoo-in to be the next Governor; but she chose Larry instead. It has been great for both them and their families, who remain good friends.

Recently, I was the guy roasted at the primary fundraiser for Senior Services, and Larry was one of the roasters along with Jack McInteer, Col. Ed Sykes, Tim Buchanan and another friend, Don Grant. We raised over $125,000 that night. Senior Services provides several programs for seniors, and most well known, for the Meals on Wheels program.

We put a lot of miles on our motorcycle, taking at least a couple of long trips each year with our RUBs buddies. We'd alternate from the East to the West coast. Once I needed to bring back one of my motorcycles from Florida, and take a new one back down that I'd bought.

I used to have a Harley Ultra Glide bike, but Renae

would develop a backache after a few hours of riding. From Miami, it was a four-hour ride down to the Keys, which was a trip we enjoyed taking. My friend had a Honda Gold Wing, and Renae could ride that all day without pain, so I sold my Harley, and got a Gold Wing. We have had them ever since. Both Wichita to Florida trips took two days, only stopping to sleep for a couple of hours. It's hard to get sleepy while riding a bike at 80 mph.

In all the trips we've taken across the years, either by ourselves or with our group, there have been a few serious accidents, but never a death. It's the fall of 2020, and I don't want there to be a first time.

I still have a bike here in Wichita, and one at the lake, but if I listen to my wife I won't have them much longer. Though I never had an accident or fell off the bike, I take a lot longer to heal these days. I think we're better off with boats.

Speaking of boats, Renae and I were out at El Dorado Lake, on the first boat we owned together and a couple of air force B-1B bombers based at McConnell AFB did a low pass over the lake. They were so low they were blasting up a rooster-tail of water off the lake. A friend of mine who had a double-decker boat actually jumped in the water thinking the plane might hit him. Everyone else was amused.

International Boat Races Weekend

We were taking a trip in our boat from Naples on the West Coast of Florida to Aventura located on the East Coast. We stopped in Key West to spend the night, but the dock master told us we would need to leave our slip the next morning as the international boat races were starting that weekend. We got up early the next morning, preparing to leave, when we noticed a good friend from Wichita, Jimmie Lee of Lee Aerospace, had his racing boat tied up right next to us. Jimmie had won the unlimited race with his Miss America racing boat a few years earlier.

When he saw us, he asked if we were there to see the races. We told him we would have liked to, if we had known, but needed to vacate our slip right away. Jimmie told us

to wait, and was gone for a short period before returning, telling us we had permission to stay for the whole show. We needed to move to a different slip, but it was a better one anyway.

After the races, and still in Key West, Jimmie asked if I would like to go for a ride in his boat, and I said yes. We idled out, and another racing boat came up alongside. Jimmie said he knew this other boat was faster than his but thought he could still beat it. The race was on. The water was rough, so Jimmie had to work the throttles. Because of his skills, we beat the other boat badly. Our GPS showed our speed at 144 knots, about 165 miles per hour. We went back in and the other guy wouldn't give up, his pride wouldn't let him. He told Jimmie he couldn't beat him again, so out we went and at 144 knots again; we outran the other guy, AGAIN. Even my hairdresser couldn't get my hair back in shape after those rides.

Watch Your Wake

Aircraft generate wake turbulence that can be deadly for other aircraft. The bigger the plane the more wake turbulence it can generate. But boats also create a wake as they travel through the water and their wake can cause damage to others.

While Renae and I were living in Florida we owned a 45 foot Sunseeker boat. One afternoon we decided to take the boat to Fort Lauderdale and have lunch at one of our favorite on-the-water restaurants. We left Aventura (North Miami Beach) for a leisurely cruise up the intercoastal waterway. There are several places on the intercoastal that are no-wake or minimal-wake zones and some of the zones are more restrictive at different times of the year. This is to try and protect the Manatees from prop injuries. We were in what we thought was a minimum-wake zone and were going quite slow when a 'Fish and Feathers' (wildlife) patrol boat stopped us and yelled that we were making a wake in a no wake zone. One of the two officers told me that once I get up to the next sign, about a quarter of a mile away, I could "bump it up" to a minimum wake. I thanked them and went on wakeless. When I got to the next sign,

I bumped it up slightly knowing the officers were still behind me. Surprisingly, they turned on their lights and siren and stopped us again. When I asked what was wrong, they said I was making a wake and it was the time of the year when the area was restricted to no wake. My pleas to the officer who said I could bump it up fell on deaf ears. One young officer boarded our boat did a complete inspection then wrote us a $500 ticket for making a wake. Keep in mind these charges were Federal charges and to pay the ticket was to admit to a Federal crime. While he had us stopped, Renae went to the controls and started the boat and the officer got quite angry. Renae then pointed to the rocks on the shore as we were about to drift into them. The officer was embarrassed at his stupidity and if he wasn't, he should have been. I think that had a lot to do with him writing the ticket.

Renae and I went to our court date and found about a dozen other no wake "criminals" wanting to protest their tickets. The Judges clerk came out before court and said if anyone wanted to settle their ticket before court started, she would take $250 versus the $500 fine. The problem was, by doing this, you had to admit you were guilty and it would go on your record. There were two of us that refused the deal and went in to the hearing. The judge seemed to be a fair person as we watched several murderers, rapist and mostly drug dealers all in shackles plead their case and get stiff sentences. They kept the wake violators until the end and the judge asked the clerk if she was recommending any prison time for us. Now that will get you to thinking. I am sure that was to get our attention because we didn't settle earlier. The other case went before me and was dismissed. When it came my turn the fish and wildlife warden asked if he could have a recess as he had a film of my wake that was being held at the security entrance. The judge was about to grant that request when I told the judge I didn't' think that would be required. The judge then said, "So obviously you are pleading guilty." I said I wasn't, but perhaps after he heard what happened he would understand. The judge asked the officer for his version of the case first. The young office seemed quite nervous and had several of the facts wrong. When I was asked my version, I turned to the officer and reminded him he was under oath. I then pointed out several errors in his statement which he admitted he made. The judge asked where the other officer was who told me I could bump it up, and when he wasn't in the courtroom, the judge apologized to me and dismissed the case. Whew! From being a convicted Federal criminal to a free man felt good. Needless to say, I was very careful to try and avoid the 'Fish and Feathers' guys from that day on. With all the security clearances required in the airline, a conviction would have been a big problem. A couple of lawyers who were in the court room stopped me and asked if I was a lawyer and when I said no, they said, "Well, you ought to be!"

Almost Lost at Sea

As you know by now, I've had plenty of adventures with my wife. This one was an "Oh shucks" one, if there ever was one. We were to have a Tri-7 board meeting in Stuart, Florida. Renae and I decided to take the boat we kept at Aventura to Stuart and just stay on the boat. The internet road maps say it's about 96 miles up there via I-95N, though I recall it being longer. Anyway, we left in plenty of time to make the trip in daylight.

About 20 miles south of Stuart, and two miles off the coast, we heard a loud BANG! The boat shook. That never signals anything good, and it wasn't. I lost steering as well as the starboard engine. Opening the engine hatch, I saw that the drive shaft to that engine had broken loose. It had allowed the starboard shaft and prop to slide until the prop was lodged in the rudder! Though we were taking on water, the bilge pumps were handling it, thankfully.

I had been wise and joined Sea Tow, a company that brings boats in distress back to shore. I immediately called them on my radio. Stuart base advised me to call another city. I did. That city advised me to call Stuart. During all this, it was getting dark. These helpful souls suggested we spend the night at sea and come in the channel the next day.

We were literally out over our heads, and I'd had enough. I advised Sea Tow my next call would be to my attorney, and Stuart and the other city could argue among themselves about who was paying his fees. It wasn't long before another man got on the phone who sounded like he actually cared, and knew what he was doing. He told me to start toward the Stuart Inlet, and he'd have a rescue boat meet me just outside the Inlet.

Those inlets can be rough sailing with very powerful currents, since those baffles are how the inter-coastal waterway handles the ocean tides. Navigating was dicey, since my only means of steering and directional control was my port engine. With the rudder jammed, I would be making slow, wide, starboard (right) turns, but I would use my bow thrusters to overturn, heading way port (left), then repeat the process for the 20 or so miles I had left to go.

My bow thrusters helped during docking, so I engaged them until my boat was heading way starboard – right – then I'd shut them down and let the port engine bring us back. I repeated this process again and again. The constant situational awareness and heightened stress was tiring me.

We finally reached the rescue boat. I relaxed a little, figuring they'd tow us the rest of the way. The captain, though, said our craft was so much bigger than his, so they couldn't tow us, but he'd be right behind, following us to the dock.

That was one hairy experience that nearly scared Renae to death. It took us another hour, but we finally made it safely in, and could breathe again. Trying to steer a big boat with a single engine and bow thrusters is no picnic!

I had seen an empty slip, so I finally maneuvered our boat around to where I could back it in. I was real proud of myself at having done this on the first try—until a woman on the dock shouted, "DON'T GO ANY FURTHER! DON'T USE THAT DOCK! THERE'S SUNKEN REBAR FROM HURRICANE DAMAGE!" I found out later they'd actually been hit by two hurricanes!

Great. Just great. Now I had to see if I could do this all over again at another dock. I finally got 'er done, but when

we'd tied the boat down and got the water leak stopped, we were both exhausted. Renae was in no mood to ride back to Aventura on that boat!

Fortunately, the dock master had maintenance people who repaired the boat while we were in Stuart. They found where I'd hit a submerged 5-gallon bucket with the prop. It had then torn the driveshaft loose and let the prop punch back into the rudder, jamming it.

On the return voyage to Aventura a few days later, my brother Larry took Renae's place. On our way out of the harbor, we hit a submerged log and messed up the new props!

I was starting to believe this boating thing sucks. I did the smart thing and sold that boat as soon as reasonable after reaching Aventura, and tried to smooth things over with Renae, telling her I'd replaced it with a better one.

We're good. It's all good, right? A that point, the only boat Renae ever wanted to be on again was one that had a butler, bringing food and drinks.

The Admirals and USS Enterprise

Mickey Markoff was the director of the Fort Lauderdale Air and Sea show for years. The military played a big role in the performances and it was known as a great annual event. One year Mickey called me in a bit of a panic, saying his fireworks sponsor had just withdrawn their support. I agreed to have Ryan International Airlines fund the fireworks. Come to find out, several of our pilots had been participating in the show and were surprised and pleased to see me there, and that we were a sponsor.

Later, Mickey invited us to join him for dinner on a Navy destroyer that was tied up next to the USS Cole. He told us the Navy controlled the seating, not him. Lo and behold, Renae and I were seated at the Admiral's table! We were seated with three admirals, and one of them was Admiral James G. Stavridis, Captain of the nuclear-powered aircraft carrier USS Enterprise and Commander of the Fifth Fleet.

That was on May 1, 2003, the same night President George W. Bush was landing on the aircraft carrier USS

Abraham Lincoln, moored just off San Diego, California. Yes, the one of "MISSION ACCOMPLISHED" fame. The press, of course, took this to mean the war in Iraq was over, when in fact the banner was put up by the crew for the mission they had just accomplished, and had nothing to do with Iraq.

The topic of conversation around our table was centered on Bush landing on a carrier. Would it be an old salt flying with him or a young tiger? What wire would they catch on the tail hook, as there are multiple cables? It was the typical buzz of US Navy fliers, only this wasn't a movie script, it was the real thing.

In the middle of our dinner a young seaman came up and whispered in Stavridis' ear. The Admiral then promptly announced, "The President's on board and all is well."

The USS Enterprise

The party was on in earnest! We talked and had a great time. The admiral asked if I'd ever been on an aircraft carrier. When I replied I had not, he asked if I would like to go sometime, to which I replied, "You bet!"

Exploring the USS Enterprise

I received an e-mail inviting me to spend three days and two nights on the USS Enterprise. I jumped at the chance, and the Admiral set a date. I was told where and when to show up, and that they would fly me out to the carrier, as it was conducting sea trials after being in dry dock for repairs.

When the day came, I boarded a twin-engine COD, one of the Navy's unsung workhorses, and flew with the four other guests, for about an hour, to an unknown location

before seeing the carrier group. On the way in, I saw a submarine off the back of the ship.

When we landed, the Admiral himself was there to greet us. When I mentioned we had seen the sub, he asked where we had spotted it because part of their mission was to find it. What an experience!

I was able to tour the carrier; go everywhere and see everything. I toured the launching pad, as well as the landing area. They even let me make the ship's announcement at the start of one day. I read off a card, and reminded every person on the ship what their duties were, along with the do's and don'ts of the day. Sleeping was tough, though, because the Enterprise was conducting nonstop air operations, launching and recovering all night. It was too short a time! The third day, they flew us back to the coast.

True confession: With as much flying as I'd done, I thought when we launched, the engines had quit; we were catapulted so fast! It became extremely quiet until the noise caught up with us. I can tell you, I had a renewed appreciation and awe for those young pros that fly off our Navy's carriers.

I have stayed in touch with Admiral Stavridis over the years. He was given command of the US Southern Command in 2006, and in July of '09, was promoted to NATO Supreme Allied Commander Europe (SACEUR), until his retirement in 2013. The framed pictures the admiral sent of my experience on the Enterprise remain treasures on my wall.

Safety and Tragedy

Atlas Air Crash

Atlas Air was a successful cargo carrier which operated several B-747s.

Their owner, Michael Chowdry, flew to Wichita in his restored DC-3 and met with me to discuss the possibility of buying Ryan International Airlines because he needed to show his stockholders steady growth of his company. Michael also had a Boeing Business Jet which was nothing short of spectacular! I never got to fly in it, but we did have several meetings in it. It was obvious to me the Pakistani-American had a flair for his chosen field. They'd done so well, they had a public offering, and as a result had a lot of cash on hand.

In the midst of those ongoing talks, I got a call from Atlas Air, telling me Michael had just died in a plane crash while taking a Wall Street Journal reporter up in another of his aircraft collection, a Russian fighter jet, just outside of Denver. Apparently, the reporter had gotten nervous and grabbed for the wrong thing, jettisoning the canopy. With it gone, Michael slowed the jet down as much as he could, but it stalled and crashed before he could get it down.

My pilot, Kirby Spangler, and I attended the funeral in Denver, parking at Arapahoe County Airport. Since it was snowing heavily, we had our Lear 25D put in a hangar.

Kirby stayed with the Lear, and following the funeral, he asked, "Did you hear about the plane crash?" I hadn't. It was a King Air 200 like mine, parked in the hangar next to our Lear and being used by the Oklahoma State basketball team. It had been full, with ten people plus baggage, and the post-crash investigation showed the lower half of the horizontal stabilizer had a heavy sheet of ice. They also discovered some reported, but deferred, electrical problems.

The whole thing really shook Kirby up since he'd helped them load their plane just prior to takeoff.

The Cincinnati Runway Fire

One of our USPS B-727s was taking off from Cincinnati, and on takeoff had a fire warning light and bell. They aborted takeoff and pulled the fire handle to discharge the fire extinguisher into the engine. The light and bell went off for a few seconds then came back on. They ran the check list and could tell there was a fire in the cargo area.

Though they couldn't see it, they could smell the smoke. To escape the fire, they had to use the cockpit emergency rope through a side window to get out of the plane. The fire consumed the entire plane right in the middle of the runway.

Hundreds of fan blades go in a circle on a plane and that's what the air goes through to make the engines work. An engine had exploded when a turbine disk had separated, causing a catastrophic failure. It punctured the fuselage after severing the main fuel line. This put hot metal and fuel in the plane, causing a large uncontainable fire. The turbine disc holds the blades and when it cracked, one of the blades pierced the side of the airplane.

During the National Transportation Safety Board (NTSB) investigation, one of the inspectors told me our crew had performed incredibly professionally and had done everything by the book except the very last thing the captain said to his crew, "This MF is on fire! Let's get the H out of here!"

He asked if I cared if he had some fun in the pilot's interview, and I said no problem.

During the interview, they went point by point through the checklist which they verified via the cockpit voice recorder until the end when the NTSB guy asked, "Just where in the checklist is the last command you gave?"

After a pregnant pause, they realized he was joking, and all had a good laugh. That engine failure created an FAA mandate requiring more turbine blade inspections on that type of popular engine for cracks or corrosion. In aviation, we tend to learn by our accidents and mistakes. This was one of those instances that showed the FAA that those types of inspections needed to happen more frequently.

Defects, when not Revealed, can be Fatal

During our many years of operating both large and small charter airplanes, we only had one aircraft fatality. I got a call one night in 1991 saying one of the USPS DC-9s had crashed in Cleveland, and the two-pilot crew had perished. I was in disbelief when I got the call and immediately thought of their families. The entire company was devastated at the loss, all over a needless and preventable accident.

We immediately took the Lear to the crash site and found out after many days of investigation, the cause was wing clutter, which is frost or ice on the wings. The plane was checked on the ground with a de-ice truck standing by, but the ground personnel had reportedly told the pilot they did not need to be de-iced. On take off, the plane stalled and rolled to the right. When the pilot corrected the roll, the plane rolled violently to the left, inverting itself and crashing onto the runway upside down. We found out about 30 days later, this same

type of accident had happened to the DC-9 on multiple occasions. McDonnell Douglas had not warned the operators of this dangerous characteristic.

After this crash, airworthiness directives on this defect were issued and to my knowledge, no other accidents of this kind have occurred.

There have been a couple of corporate jets that have found out the hard way that they are also are susceptible to this problem. The FAA rules have always stated that no airplane is to takeoff with any wing contamination, but human judgment always comes into the equation.

It was simple to test. The solution to this was as simple as attaching a tuft of yarn or string on the top of the wing. The mechanic was required to check to see if it was frozen to the wing before takeoff.

The Runway Tragedy at the FBO

The only other fatality we had was at the FBO in the early 80s. One of our young aircraft service technicians had driven the lavatory trailer behind a four-wheel, open top vehicle we call a tug. He drove the tug under a plane. Late that night I received a call from airport security stating they had found one of our linemen laying out on the airport ramp, dead, and a tug about a quarter of a mile away next to the runway. Jack McInteer, who was president at the time, and I immediately went to the airport to investigate, but what happened was a mystery for some time. We serviced the airlines that overnighted in Wichita, and I knew he was probably servicing one of the planes. I went and looked at several planes, and when I came

PB91-910410
NTSB/AAR-91/09

NATIONAL TRANSPORTATION SAFETY BOARD
WASHINGTON, D.C. 20594

AIRCRAFT ACCIDENT REPORT

RYAN INTERNATIONAL AIRLINES
DC-9-15, N565PC
LOSS OF CONTROL ON TAKEOFF
CLEVELAND-HOPKINS INTERNATIONAL AIRPORT
CLEVELAND, OHIO
FEBRUARY 17, 1991

5499A

NTSB Accident Report

to the Continental DC-9, I found oil smudges and what looked like wipe marks across the rear belly of the plane. We determined the lineman had driven up to the plane obviously quite fast, couldn't stop, and went under the plane, crushing him. He fell off some distance away, but the tug continued all the way out to the runway. A young man with a lot of life ahead of him was unfortunately lost too soon.

As a result of this accident, we implemented new safety rules. In all our years of operations of both large and small aircraft, our safety record is second to none. We have had some close calls over the years. Almost all aviation accidents can be traced back to human error. Lack of precision can have devastating consequences and can even be deadly.

Bus on the Runway

We were the very first commercial airliner to operate in and out of the new Denver International Airport, DEN, with a USPS plane in 1995. The building of the Denver airport was quite controversial, as it was way over budget and way behind schedule. They built an automated baggage conveyor that wouldn't carry skis, believe it or not!

Sometime later, we had a close call at DEN. At the time we were flying 22 airplanes for USPS. A USPS B-727 was taxiing out at night, when an airport passenger bus moving flight crews and maintenance people around the airport ran into the nose of the plane and opened up the cockpit so bad that the co-pilot almost fell onto the runway; thankfully, her seatbelt held her in. The bus was on a taxiway not paying attention. It was the bus driver's fault.

The pilot couldn't stop the plane as the hydraulic and electrical had been severed in the crash. The plane started rolling backward with the engines running, as they couldn't shut them off. An alert Federal Express worker saw what happened, and ran out with wheel chocks to stop the plane. He kept putting them under the wheels, and the plane would jump the chocks, but slowed down enough that eventually got the plane stopped. The accident put all three crewmembers in the hospital with non-life-threatening injuries, but the B-727 was totaled. The insurance companies were then involved to figure out who pays what. We had to scrap that airplane. Before long, another replaced it. We had mail to move!

Lee Striker

One evening we were having dinner with all the ski bums at Jack DeBoer's Aspen home, which included Lee Striker of Striker Medical Supplies out of Kalamazoo. Lee was prescient that night as he remarked, "Remember – one day we may not all be here again together, because sometimes bad things happen to good people." Later that year Lee accidentally flew his Aero Commander into a box canyon and killed himself and all on board. The plane burned so badly there wasn't anything to bury. His company still lives on and seems to be doing well in the medical business. But, Lee was right, the next year he wasn't there with us.

Larry Armstrong

I had another friend from my flight instructing days at Fairfax named Larry Armstrong. Larry was an Italian young man whose family was connected to the Kansas City Mob. Larry would take me to different night clubs owned or operated by his family and, boy, did I learn a lot about life! Well, part of it, anyway.

One of the bars was a gay bar for guys, and another was a gay bar for girls. Larry would often tend bar, so I would wind up sitting at the end of the bar. If I needed to use the restroom, Larry would give me the key to the women's room at one bar, and the key to the men's room at the other. The bathrooms were generally where the people hooked up, and he was keeping me clear of any problems. One thing about it: the bouncers and guys on the door earned their keep. If a stranger came to the bar entrance, the doorman would be at the door, making it clear, "This is a private party." That always kept the gawkers out.

I suppose the most impressionable thing to me as a young kid was the number of professionals, highly paid executives, and celebrities who were not straight. I must say everyone I met was polite, courteous and considerate and part of that was probably due to my friendship with Larry as he was straight.

When I got a job in Wichita with Jack, Larry kept asking me to hire him, but I knew he wasn't experienced enough for our needs. My friend was determined, though. He eventually got himself into a Lear cockpit, but not for long. Shortly after that, Larry got killed in a Learjet crash in Detroit carrying car parts.

A guy by the name of Al Israel was operating a Lear out of KC and was using Larry as a co-pilot. They landed after shooting a low visibility approach at Detroit's downtown airport on a short runway and were fast and long. When they saw they were going to overshoot the runway, one of them, on touch down, put out the spoilers to kill lift on the wings. Then, when they tried to do a go-around, they forgot to retract the spoilers. This is the same mistake that caused the first Lear prototype to crash in Wichita while the FAA was testing the plane.

They crashed off the end of the runway, killing both of them. The one passenger in the back was critically injured, but did get out alive.

Flying requires constant attention to detail, ongoing training and recertification, situational awareness, and a knowledge of one's aircraft, including emergency procedures. I know from some of what I've shared here, it may sound like I was a bit of a daredevil. My wife knows I still am. However, you should always know your own and your airplane's limitations.

John Denver

Once while at the Learjet factory, I saw a guy who looked familiar. It was John Denver. I guess I shouldn't have been surprised, as I knew his dad, Dutch Dusseldorf. He was a Learjet captain and flew for the Lear factory. Dutch always seemed to be a very pleasant person although I never flew with him.

They were there that day picking up a Lear for John, and his dad was going to be his captain. Sadly, John eventually killed himself in an aircraft he was flying that a friend had built at home. John was out over the water when his engine ran out of fuel. He had fuel in another tank, but was unfamiliar with the plane, so crashed and perished. A sad ending to a great performer. An error in a switch setting resulted in tragic consequences.

Dead Reckoning

I had a couple of other friends who killed themselves in plane crashes by ferrying aircraft overseas. Flo-Air was a company I eventually bought, which was in the business of tanking and equipping planes to be flown overseas or to Hawaii.

This was long before GPS or any satellite navigation. Most of it was by what we call dead reckoning, and after making a few of those flights, I think I know why they named it that. The world's oceans are big to begin with.

When you are out over the ocean, it becomes a huge body of water and finding an island where one can refuel is tricky, and sometimes a matter of pure luck. The smallest miscalculation, either of the winds, fuel burn or direction, could be, and often was, fatal.

Mark Goldstein

A couple of years ago a good friend of mine, Mark Goldstein, was ferrying a King Air 200 to Mena, Arkansas, for refurbishing. Mark had retired a year earlier after 17 years as an air traffic controller and loved to fly.

Renae and I were at a restaurant about 20 miles away when some of my friends started calling to see if I was OK. After the third call I asked why everyone was checking on me. They said the news was reporting that a King Air 200 had just crashed at the Wichita main airport, had hit one of the FlightSafety Training buildings, and there were several deaths.

We knew Mark was supposed to be taking a King Air 200 that morning to Arkansas. Brian Denny, a pilot friend, made several calls and figured without a doubt, it was Mark. We quickly headed to the airport, where the building was still burning.

I have served on that Airport Advisory Commission, so I knew the safety officers. When we told them we knew who the pilot was, they took us to the FBI tent where several law enforcement groups were meeting. We listened to the ATC tapes and told them we knew it was Mark, and they said they suspected as much but were not sure. Actually, the tower personnel knew for sure it was Mark, but weren't allowed to say anything.

Mark had flown with me several times and I sent him to King Air School a couple of times. In fact, he'd attended flight school just the week before for his King Air 350 type rating. He was single but dating a very nice woman. My friend's body remained on top of the building for a couple of days until recovery crews could collapse some of the teetering, unstable walls that remained.

Renae had the unenviable task of calling Mark's parents in Florida and giving them the bad news. She also talked to Mark's sister, who was shocked and in disbelief. The irony of this story is that three people were killed in the flight simulator. The instructor who jumped from the simulator in the building that was hit, broke his leg, but crawled to safety.

Think about it.

You attend FlightSafety school to become a better pilot and wind up getting killed in the simulator. How ironic is that?

Mark was a caring, careful flier. His biggest regret would have been that others got hurt and killed because of his accident. We know the left engine lost power on takeoff because he was on tape, reporting that to the tower. Why he didn't abort or was unable to fly on the good engine is still unknown. Either action would have saved his and the others' lives.

The Heart Attack

My brother Larry had a good friend who owned a Stearman and was flying a cross-country, stopping several places to raise money for a charity. He took a doctor friend with him, and while in Colorado on a flight, he slumped over the stick, and the doctor could tell something was wrong.

The pilot regained enough of his senses to bring the plane in flat. However, when it hit the ground it burst into flames. The doctor was injured, but managed to crawl out to safety. Larry's friend perished. It was surmised he had a heart attack but was determined not to crash, and saved the doctor's life by getting the plane on the ground, despite the fire.

And the Stories Continue

The guy was trying to sell insider information to make a profit. It wasn't right and I wasn't buying.

The Boeing Engine Foil

While operating my first airline, a nice looking man, probably in his early thirties, came into my second story office at Mid-Continent Airport. He asked if I would grant him a meeting, as he did not have an appointment. I said, "Sure."

He asked, "Would you like to make a lot of money?

I said, "Wouldn't we all?"

He told me he worked for Boeing, and that all the KC-135 tankers were going to be re-engined with fan jet engines, and he knew where every engine eligible for this retrofit was located in the world. He further explained that most were on older DC-8s that were going to be retired. I asked, "What is your plan?"

He said with my help and some money, we could get options to buy most, if not all the engines, and when Boeing got the contract from the military, we could mark them up and make a lot of money. I told him that sounded if not illegal, at least immoral, since he was working for Boeing.

He said he had retired from the military and had watched a lot of politicians get rich. This was his opportunity. I got his name and phone number and told him I would get back to him. Bev Lancaster at Boeing and I had become friends, just as I had with Lionel Alford the head of Boeing Military, Wichita. I told him about my conversation. He told me not to worry about it saying no one could do what he was suggesting.

Bev called me a couple of days later and asked if the Boeing security people could come to my office and meet with me. I agreed. They explained that the guy, indeed, had the data to pull off what he had suggested, and wanted to know if I would help them catch him in the act. I agreed and set up another meeting at my office, wearing a wire. They wanted me to let him make his pitch again, then have him leave. They would arrest him in the parking lot, as they didn't want him to know I was the one who tipped them off, concerned he might seek revenge on me.

He came to my office, with his files on every engine owner and location. After the meeting, he left, and I waited for some time. I finally went downstairs, and security said he never came out.

They started a search of the building and found him in the men's room standing on top of a toilet, so they couldn't see his feet. He told them when he was getting ready to leave, he saw his boss out in our parking lot, so he ducked into the rest room and hid.

I was told later that they fired him. Although I think they could have put him in jail, they let him off easy. Wearing a wire was eerie. Ever since, I have a different feeling than most when I see people on TV or in a movie, wearing a wire.

Sabotage Stinks

During the years we flew for Emery, operated our charter services, and ran the FBO, we made a lot of friends and were blessed to be paid well for our services. We'd outgrown the building we had purchased from Air Midwest Airlines just adjacent to the ICT airport. Although we had offices in both Indianapolis, and Dayton, Ohio, which was Emery's sort center, we needed a lot more space. We did have space in most of the airports we operated out of, primarily for our crews and maintenance personnel, but also including ticket counter space for our charter operations.

In downtown Wichita, we bought the old telephone company's computer center on 2nd and Main and remodeled both floors, each one was 40,000 square feet. We also completely renovated the basement, converting it into indoor parking. We'd been so busy we had scant time to oversee the FBO. We talked with Stan Roth from Newton, which is about 20 miles north of Wichita. Stan was buying, updating and selling mostly larger corporate aircraft, and agreed our FBO would suit his needs. He bought it and moved some of his Newton operations to Wichita.

Prior to Stan buying our FBO, we had fired a couple of maintenance people who did not meet our standards of quality. For whatever reason, Stan had hired both of the people we had fired. Consequently, the minute Stan moved his operation from Newton to Wichita, these two characters set out to do their best to poison our personal and professional relationship with him.

We'd contracted with Stan to do all our B-727 support while our planes were in Wichita, plus we kept a large aircraft inventory in leased space at the FBO. One day, Stan called and said he needed me to come out there, so he could show me a problem. I dropped what I was doing, and went. What he showed me was the cistern we'd built, back when servicing the major airlines, to temporarily store waste from the lavatory trucks. We had a septic service that regularly came and pumped all of the waste out.

One of the critters I'd fired had told Stan that we were now dumping our used oil and solvents. Talk about disgusted. These vindictive types never seem to think things through, do they? This wasn't the first lie and deception they had tried against me with Stan.

I immediately called for a chemical analysis of samples to be taken. They found nothing more than a lot of dirty water.

I felt uncomfortable having the employees we fired service, store or be around my planes. I worked out a deal with Midwest Corporate Jet's owner Marvin Autry, to move my corporate planes to Jabara Airport and have them do our service. Marvin and I were always fierce competitors, always friends, and I trusted him. I still have my King Air Super 200 there. Sadly, Marvin died a few years ago, but his beautiful and talented wife Barbara still runs the FBO, and is in fact, expanding the operations.

A short time after I made the switch, I received a call that Stan had killed himself and his brother while flying a Rockwell Sabreliner, trying to do a loop, but hitting the ground before they could pull out. The weather was clear, and later investigation indicated Stan was demonstrating a Chandelle maneuver to his brother. On the top side, instead of rolling level at the higher altitude, Stan let the plane roll, inverted. Even then, being just above stall speed, if he'd had a hundred more feet of altitude, he could have still recovered.

At Stan's funeral, his banker, Jim Taylor, asked his wife what he could do for her. Jim later told me how that is such a common thing to say at a funeral, and little did he know she was going to take him up on his offer. She said she needed him to operate the FBO. He did just that, setting up Executive AirShares, a fractional ownership operation that still flies several aircraft at this writing. The FBO remains today as a private maintenance and storage hangar operation.

The B-727 Bright Idea

Sometime after Jack DeBoer had sold his interest in the FBO, he and his wife Marilyn took an around the world pleasure trip. Jack came back with the idea of setting up an exclusive B-727 airplane with sixty seats to take around the world trips for high paying passengers. I told Jack I didn't think the idea would work, as he would be selling the seats and needed to be a FAA Part 121 operator, neither of which was easy or cheap. Jack ignored me and purchased a B-727 from TWA out of Kansas City. He paid way too much money, in my opinion, but that didn't matter much to Jack at the time.

He hired Andy Camarada, to put his 121 operation together. They had the plane taken to a shop in Florida to have it modified; when he went to pick it up, his bill was 10 million dollars. That was more than what Jack had paid for the plane.

I told Jack I would sell him my entire B-727 book and manuals already approved by our local FAA for $50,000. Andy scoffed at the idea, reminding me that he was a former Continental Airline captain, and stating that this was no big deal for him. Over a year later, and several million dollars before they got their certificate, I am sure they looked at that decision differently.

They never flew the plane around the world. Their first charter trip, many months later, was scheduled to go to New York, pick up a wedding party, and take them to Italy. En route, the number three engine literally exploded, knocking out the number two engine and puncturing the fuselage in several places. They had to make an emergency, one engine landing and found more than a million dollars' worth of damage. In addition, they had to charter another plane to take their trip. Talk about bad luck and wasted money in starting an airline.

Starting and running an airline is a very expensive and time-consuming proposition. Some new operators get lulled into thinking they know what it is costs to operate until they hit a heavy maintenance requirement or have a serious mechanical failure. Things such as C and D checks may cost well over a million dollars to accomplish, and take several weeks. Downtime on an airplane is very costly. Over the years we were often asked to help someone start their own airline; but once we showed them the real costs and complexity, they usually passed. Plus, most of them didn't have the amount of money needed.

Alcohol and Airplanes Don't Mix

I can't repeat this phrase enough… "The pilot is always the first one at the scene of the accident."

I never drank alcohol a minimum of 12 hours before a flight and that is the rule we had for our flight crews, including flight attendants. The FAA's rule is eight hours, but most airlines have a 24-hour rule, which I think does more harm than good. It induces a lot of pilots to break that rule, and if you are going to break a rule, where do you draw the line? Make it safe and reasonable and enforce it. Of course, they didn't ask me.

At one time, we had to undergo mandatory drug and alcohol testing on 50% of our flight crews each year. Then it was reduced to 25% each year. We also had to do surprise random breathalyzer tests on flight crews, just as they were getting on the plane prior to a flight. We never caught one of our crew members drinking or using drugs, but we did catch a few mechanics.

Other airlines did catch several who were beyond the limit, which is basically zero prior to a flight. When the FAA came out with the mandatory testing requirements, the committee that represented the pilots came to Wichita and we did a drinking test. We had all kinds of alcohol and a breathalyzers. We had different people drink different amounts and types of alcohol to see how long it took to be legal to fly.

We were stunned to find out how long it takes for alcohol to leave your system! One guy was still legally drunk the next morning; this helped our pilots better understand the risks of drinking.

There were a couple of occasions when a passenger getting on the plane had asked the pilot if he or she had been drinking. When this happened, the pilot was required to immediately go to the nearest hospital and have a blood test regardless. This usually delays the flight for at least an hour, and the person causing the delay is not a very popular passenger.

People often ask if pilots feel a tremendous amount of responsibility. I always tell them, "The pilot's always the first one at the scene of the accident." In other words, if we take care of ourselves, we're not going to hurt anybody else.

The Fanatic

Ray Thomas our VP of Maintenance had to fire one employee for bringing a fetus to work in a bottle and showing it to our single moms. The guy had continually pulled stunts similar to this one. He was an anti-abortion fanatic, who was forcing his ideas on our female employees. Because a person believes something doesn't make it right, and we shouldn't try to force our beliefs on other people.

Dialogue is for building trust, even when ideas are different. We would take our differences of opinion and debate them and come up with something that was workable for all. It was okay to disagree, but not okay to be disagreeable.

That guy later was hired by the FAA and became our chief maintenance inspector. I complained that he was sabotaging our operations, as he disliked Ray so much. The problems kept happening, so sometime later we set a trap for him. He fell into it, and the FAA couldn't deny what he had been doing. Like most government agencies, they didn't fire him, but put him on a different assignment.

A second guy who used to fly my King Air, who I felt wasn't strong enough to fly the Lear I was buying, also got hired by the FAA and went on to become our chief A-320 flight examiner. At least he didn't have an axe to grind. He was a standup guy and very inexperienced, yet, he was the guy who was supposed to tell us how to operate our large jets safely. Go figure.

The Bomb Scare

One day we received a very unsettling call from an unknown person at our airline headquarters. The voice said, "You've got a bomb in your office!" and hung up. To evacuate would have been a big deal, but to have a bomb go off would be an even bigger one!

We probably had more than 30 planes in the sky when we got that call, and we needed to be able to stay in touch for many reasons. We had to flight dispatch each plane, give flight releases, weather and any rerouting necessary. Security immediately wanted to call in the dogs and alert all the employees. A quick decision had to be made. They came to Renae and asked what to do. She immediately went to the first floor, where the company that operated our phone service was located. She asked them to trace the call. At first they refused, but she explained the seriousness of the situation and assured them she'd be personally responsible if anyone were to be held liable.

A short time later the phone company's boss came to Renae and said he couldn't tell us who, but he could give her some hints, and if she guessed, he could confirm. He said it wasn't a Ryan employee, but someone who worked in the building with us. Renae figured out it was the teenage son of one of Emery Air Freight's female accountants, who had made the call. In the FBI investigation, the boy said he just wanted his mother to be able to come home. We filed no charges and told Emery we did not want a good worker to lose her job over something an airheaded kid had done.

I'm not sure what motivated him to behave this way... broken families can result in bad actions. I didn't know the young man, but I wonder how he felt being interviewed by the FBI. I hope the incident brought them closer, and that he received the attention he really needed, in a positive way. Young or old, our actions have consequences.

The Aventura Con Job

After we sold the airline the second time, we bought a two-story penthouse condo that was still under construction in Aventura, in North Miami Beach. Most are delivered "designer-ready," which means you have very little finishes included.

Because they really wanted to get this penthouse sold, I got them to agree to finish the condo as part of our deal, so we had to pick out the flooring and some other things to ensure the finished product was right. A few months before we were to move in, the builder sent a note saying they would be willing to finish out our condo for another $600,000. It should have been zero!

We thought this was a mistake and contacted the developer, who said they had not agreed to finish out our condo. We told them we had the contract and went to meet with the main developers in Naples, Florida, where they were headquartered. We showed them our contract, and they showed us the one that the salespeople in Aventura had given them. They were totally different!

I was in Ireland at the time, so when the salesman said they had agreed to all our terms, I told Renae to go ahead and sign. The sales team lied and cheated Renae, giving her an entirely different contract to sign, when he told her it was the one we had negotiated.

Fortunately, we had saved the contract we had agreed on. We didn't mess around. We immediately hired a lawyer and sued the developer. In response, they quickly admitted fraud by the salesman and agreed to finish our apartment. They'd apparently pulled that scam before.

In the interim, since we had already sold the condo we were living in, we moved into a guest room in our new building until they completed our new home. They did an excellent job, and we wound up with a beautiful condo we loved. We had a boat and boat slip right outside the building. We sold all of our Florida holdings in 2010, when we received custody of our granddaughter and her older brother, and moved back to Wichita, the place I call home.

Shaken Up in San Francisco

While I had the charter business, several Wichita businesspeople and I were invited to ride along in a KC-135 tanker to California. It was a fairly routine flight, during which we did some aerial refueling. Landing at the California air base, it felt like the aircraft was moving sideways. In my experience, Boeing 707 airplanes don't usually do that. The KC-135 is basically a Boeing 707 modified to be a tanker, but fly the same.

I shrugged it off; they got us to our hotel, and I flipped on the TV while trying to call home. The phone kept repeating the message that all lines were busy, and to please try again later. I hung up, and finally focused on the TV. It looked like one of those Japanese horror movies!

A slab on the Golden Gate Bridge had collapsed, and there was a fire on it somewhere. As the camera shifted, it showed major fires around the San Francisco Wharf area and a huge section of collapsed freeway. It finally clicked: San Francisco had experienced a major earthquake that had occurred at exactly the same time we had landed.

One of our charter jets was in San Francisco with a client who was there to watch a World Series game. They were forced to postpone the game from October 17th to the 27th.

Right after the quake, car travel was almost impossible. Somehow, our passengers made it to the airport and our Lear eventually got out safely, though it had to dodge cracks in the runway and taxiways. The group that flew out on the KC-135 stayed there a couple of days and then flew back to McConnell Air Force Base, shaken up but unharmed.

The Taiwanese Quake

Of course, believing in the scientific method, I had to try another quake, just to be sure. This one happened to be in Taiwan. I was on my way to Koahsiung to a meeting with one of our Guam/Saipan B-727 fish customers. Needing to spend the night in Taipei, as I had an early flight out the next morning, I booked a room in the Hilton, and they put me on the top floor, fifteen stories up.

Long day, late-night check-in, me tired: you know the drill. So, the bed shaking took a while to wake me up. I knew I hadn't paid extra for a vibrating mattress, so I figured maybe I'd had one too many drinks. I turned on the bedside lamp and noticed my clothes hanging in the closet were swinging back and forth. Last I checked, they didn't normally do that. It took me a minute or two to realize I wasn't dreaming but was smack in the middle of another earthquake!

I looked out the window, and there was no traffic on the highways at all. When the sun came up, I went downstairs. Everyone was excitedly talking about the quake and all the damage caused. The hotel manager told me the Hilton had been built on giant springs in anticipation of just such a possibility, which is why I had such an interesting ride on the top floor.

Wow, what a helpless feeling! What's a guy supposed to do? Stay huddled under the covers? Try to get down 15 flights of stairs, hide in a closet, what? A chute would've been welcome. Okay. I've decided two earthquakes is enough. I'm a believer. Someone else can enjoy them from now on.

The next day, my flight to Koahsiung ran about an hour late because they needed to clear the runway of all obstacles and check it for damage. But we did get airborne. Visiting the fish market in Koahsiung was very interesting.

Lots of coordinated chaos and very expensive, exotic fish in all sizes and shapes. My customer, Chairman Woo, also had a fish hatchery with millions of fish being raised for harvest. Visiting that fish farm was quite interesting, especially during feeding time.

Sadly, the sun still sets at two in the afternoon, in the polluted haze of Taiwan. Unless, or until, we can get the Asian nations to clear up the air, it is futile for us to continue to hurt our economy and people with unwise pollution restrictions. I am in total favor of clean water and air but think some of the ways we strive to accomplish this is hurting us more than helping.

Paris

Aero Systems, headquartered in Miami, and based at MIA, was an aircraft parts company we purchased. The previous owner, Ed Holmes, was someone I met during the around the world speed record attempt and became a friend. He had a great relationship with the Disney people in Florida. On one trip to the Paris Airshow, Disney put us up overnight in the Cinderella Suite, which is right over Main Street in Disneyland. The Disney characters all visited us, and one of their composers wrote some music for Renae to play, since they found out her degree was in music and knew she played a piano as well as she does. Renae regularly plays the piano at our church in Wichita and at our Grand Lake home. The Disney people know how to do things right.

While in Paris, we went out on the town with a tour, and they took a group of us to a racy night club featuring dancers and comedians. They talked Doug Jackson up on stage and had a lot of fun making a total fool out of him. We knew it was part of the act, and they'd done it plenty of times before. The problem arose when they were done, and they asked him his name. With a huge grin, he proudly exclaimed, "I'm Ron Ryan from Wichita, Kansas!"

Spectacular Light

Renae and I were coming back from one of our many Florida trips on a very clear day. I was flying the Lear, and we were at 45,000 feet headed back to Wichita. While passing over Central Florida, we were able to see Cape Kennedy quite clear. ATC told us there was going to be a shuttle launch.

When it blasted off, the sight from that altitude was spectacular. We were able to watch the launch until it was who-knows-how-far in space. I just know we gawked like a couple of little kids until it was out of sight. That's a once-in-a-lifetime event I will never forget!

Another spectacular sight is seeing the Northern Lights from 45,000 feet. I have seen them often and never stop being amazed at their beauty. I have also seen sparks jumping off the tip tanks of the Lear, as well as blue flames coming out in front of the windscreen on the Lear while flying through precipitation. It is static electricity being discharged. We have static wicks on the trailing edges of the wings, but sometimes it builds up to where they can't discharge it all. It is beautiful and scary, and something most people have never witnessed.

One time Kirby Spangler, my corporate pilot now deceased, was ferrying the Lear to the Lake to pick up Renae and me, and there was a thunderstorm a couple of miles from the airport. Just as Kirby lifted off, he took a direct lighting strike. He came to the lake and we found several small pin holes burnt into the skin of the plane, plus we had to change out several pieces of electronics when we got back to Wichita. Kirby said only he, and whoever did his laundry, would know how scary that was.

Aviation Friends

As I've mentioned throughout this book, I've been blessed with many friends and known some great people. Never wanting to leave anyone out, I'm saying thanks to everyone who ever worked with or for me, and to all those who have been in my life.

An Admired Friend, Bob Hoover

I was very fortunate to have known and flown with Bob Hoover, one of the greatest pilots God ever created. He was 6 foot 3 inches tall, and about 140 pounds. Known as the Best Aerobatic Pilot in the World, he was a gentle soul. He always wore a panama hat and a jumpsuit and could tell great stories in his quiet way, and he always treated you like you were his best friend.

Bob had a Sabreliner he would use in his air shows, as well as a Rockwell Shrike Commander. In his later years when Bob was performing, a couple of FAA examiners were watching and telling each other they thought Bob was too old to be doing air stunts. On their own, they denied giving his medical certificate to him.

Famous lawyer F. Lee Bailey handled Bob's case. One of the inspectors admitted what they had done, and the FAA gave Bob back his medical. As I've mentioned previously, Clay Lacy is a Wichita-born aviator who runs Clay Lacy Aviation at Van Nuys Airport. He, Tim Bonnell, who owned Professional Insurance Management, and I were involved

Renae Ryan, Bob Hoover and Ron Ryan

128

in getting Bob's medical back. Bob told me he would know before anyone else when his skills started slipping, and he would hang it up without anyone telling him to do so.

Evergreen Airlines had been sponsoring Bob before this happened. I had taken away from Evergreen their biggest postal flying contract, so Evergreen refused to continue to sponsor Bob. So I did, under the name Ryan International Airlines. And we sponsored Bob until he decided to quit flying air shows.

Breaking the Sound Barrier

In his early Air Force test pilot days, Bob flew with Chuck Yeager, who was the first man to break the sound barrier. Bob was scheduled to fly that flight, but a few days earlier, he buzzed the nearby town and got in trouble with the commander, so Chuck was asked to fly the Bell experimental aircraft.

The story is harrowing. As Chuck Yeager went through the sound barrier, he lost altitude control. When he pulled back on the stick, the plane's nose went down versus the up he wanted. He then reversed his actions, and when he put the yoke down, the plane's nose went up, and he was able to control the flight by reversing control inputs. We were just learning about the shock wave that breaking the sound barrier produces. We lost several good airmen before we had discovered this.

Bob's 90th Birthday

A group of Bob Hoover's friends decided to give him a 90th birthday party in Fredericksburg, Texas, the home of the Navy's combat museum. I flew down, and once Renae and I landed, they said a plane was waiting on us to fly us to another location where many top aviators including several astronauts, Herb Kelleher, numerous celebrities, and even the governor of Texas were in attendance. This was at a private airstrip where some of the flyers put on an airshow. We later flew back to Fredericksburg and had a party there.

The Ryan International Airlines name is still on Bob's Shrike Commander that hangs in the Smithsonian Aviation Museum. Bob was not only a good pilot, but one of the most gracious people you could ever meet. He had Tim and me out to his house for dinner several times. We really enjoyed hearing him tell us about his flying adventures, and he had a lot of them. His wife, Colleen, was a superstar to put up with a pilot's life as many years as she did.

Whenever Bob would show up anywhere, he would draw a crowd of admirers. He was one of the aviation world's giants. It was my honor to know him. Bob died in 2016, and he is sorely missed.

High Altitude Flying

High altitude flying was also another expensive and costly lesson we needed to learn. In the Lear or any airplane at 41,000 feet, if you lose pressurization you have less than 10 SECONDS to get your O2 pressurized mask on and get the plane headed down fast, very fast. They call these few seconds the time of useful consciousness. You would think you could hold your breath longer than that but because the pressure on the outside of your body is less than the pressure inside your body, all the O2 is pushed out, creating hypoxia and death. The mask in an airliner will only support life below around 30,000 feet depending on the individual. A famous golfer, Payne Stewart, lost his life in a Lear where the pressurization failed for some reason, and the autopilot flew the plane until it ran out of fuel.

Unfortunately, hypoxia gives you a false sense of security almost like being drunk, and a pilot can make some very bad decisions if they allow the onset of hypoxia. Although there may have been some sort of malfunction, almost certainly, this was a situation mishandled by the crew. My personal feeling is they failed to turn on the pressure switches before takeoff. Easy to do but the plane has warning horns, but my guess is they mistook the altitude warning horn for the overspeed horn and continued to climb. A fatal mistake.

Another costly lesson was the growing of fungus in jet fuel at high altitudes and low temperatures. Several Air Force airplanes crashed before they discovered this fungus was plugging up the fuel filters. We now add an anti-bacteria solution to all jet fuels to prevent this problem, even in corporate jets.

Good Ol' Ray Thomas

Ray was a very integral part of our success. You've heard me speak of our chief of maintenance. Well, he was a short, small guy who was a heavy smoker. We wouldn't allow any smoking in our building, so he and the other smokers would go outside the front door to smoke.

Renae found an old toilet someplace and placed it outside the door with a sign, "PUT YOUR BUTTS HERE." We couldn't discriminate against smokers in Ohio or Indiana but wouldn't hire smokers in Kansas. I had a deal where I would pay $500 to any of my employees who smoked. The catch was if they were ever got caught smoking, they owed me $1,000. I had several employees who took me up on the offer, but I never had to try and collect from anyone who was caught smoking. I think word got around I wasn't just being a grinch, but that I really cared about my people.

I even offered Ray $10,000 to quit smoking, but he didn't, and died a horrible death from emphysema and lung cancer. Ray is sorely missed, and I remain grateful for his contributions to my business and life.

Tora, Tora, Tora

Doug Jackson was an important person in our company; between his work and his hobbies, there were always adventures. Doug's dad was an airline pilot, so Doug grew up knowing airplanes. One of Doug's stories was when he was about six years old, his dad let him fly to Hawaii on a flight where his dad was the Captain. During the flight, Doug had spent some time in the cockpit and, when returning to his seat, started crying. When people asked what was wrong, Doug said they were going to crash as they didn't have enough fuel to get to Hawaii. After the commotion finally settled down, Doug's dad was quite unhappy with him, but allowed him to grow up. I imagine there were some very uncomfortable passengers on that flight.

Ron & Renae Ryan with "Tora, Tora, Tora" Plane

Doug Jackson, who in addition to buying and selling corporate jet aircraft, was also buying and fixing up and selling vintage aircraft. He bought a couple of Stearmans and was able to sell them quickly. He bought a T-6 that was painted up like a Japanese Zero. In fact, it was the lead aircraft in the movie "Tora, Tora, Tora". Doug would fly in airshows all over the country and said he hated the fact that he was the guy who always got shot down. Sadly, Doug died from cancer just a few years ago. I tell a lot of people none of us are going to get out of this world alive, so we need to be sure we are at peace with our Maker.

Kirby Spangler, Fond Memories

I still own and fly a King Air 200. This is a twin-engine turbo prop aircraft that can be flown by a single pilot. I have a full-time captain who usually goes with me when I use the plane. His name is J.D. Ratts, and he has been with me for about seven years.

I had a previous pilot for my Lears and King Airs, Kirby Spangler. He had a lovely wife and daughter. I had him because he was able to fly several planes. Over the years, I had several different aircraft types at different times. If someone came along and thought my plane was worth more than I did, I'd sell it and buy another one. Kirby's dad was a test pilot for Beech Aircraft, so Kirby grew up around airplanes and knew them well.

I had a different pilot flying the King Air when I bought the Lear. I was concerned the pilot I had couldn't learn the Lear as fast as I needed, so it worked out well when that pilot went to work for our local FAA. Surprisingly enough, he later became our primary overseer for our Airbus A-320 program. We used our Lear a lot to run parts and mechanics all over the world to assist in any broken airplanes. We had such tight schedules and flew so many hours, a mechanical delay created long-term nightmares.

We used to keep about $40,000 cash at the office, so if Kirby had to go rescue a broken airplane, he could take enough money to pay for whatever he needed. That may sound like overkill, but generally where he had to go was out of the country and usually the calls for help came in the middle of the night.

I trained Kirby to fly the Lear and sent him to Flight Safety to get his type rating. The afternoon Kirby was awarded his license to fly the Lear, I told him I had forgotten something at the lake and needed him to go with us to pick it up. Renae asked me what was it that I "forgot," and

I told her I wanted to see how Kirby would handle a 3800 foot runway in a Learjet.

In other words, I was being sneaky.

Kirby was fantastic and did a great job. The man had "The Touch." He flew for the our Airline, as a corporate pilot, as well as for me. He had the opportunity to go to flight school for the big planes but elected to continue to fly the corporate planes. We did give him a pilot seniority number in case he ever changed his mind.

Long before Kirby got sick, he was teaching my wife not only how to fly, but also land both the Lear as well as the King Air. She handled it well, which gave me comfort when just the two of us were flying. If something happened to me, she could get the plane down safely. I was convinced even though I had taught a lot of people how to fly trying to teach one's wife is not a good idea.

That was Kirby.

After returning one day from delivering a plane to Mexico, Kirby had a terrible headache and went to the doctor. The diagnosis was brain cancer. They gave him about 18 months to live! He not only lost his flight physical, but couldn't even fly commercially due to pressure changes in his head.

You've got to know what a punch in the gut that is to a man who loves to fly. If ever I knew a born pilot, it was Kirby Spangler.

He asked me if I thought he should fight the cancer. I said it was up to him but if it were me, I would fight it. He did fight the disease. He had at least two serious brain operations in Houston, Texas, and although I offered to fly him, he had to drive because of pressure issues.

He seemed to be functioning well up until about six weeks before he died. Once he knew he had been diagnosed with terminal cancer, he asked me if I'd have my brother Larry come and talk with him. Larry did come, and Kirby became a Christian who handled his disease and remaining days with courage and dignity.

During his illness, he helped me along with the assistance of another great pilot, Brian Denny, to keep up the records on my plane, as well as to help me find the King Air 200 I now own. He previously helped me sell the Lear 25D that I owned. Kirby also found J.D. Ratts, my current pilot, and helped some of my business friends find good pilots for their planes. He was on our payroll up until the day he died.

High Flying with Clay Lacy

As a pilot, Clay Lacy provided some of the highlights of my life. With him, we set the Around the World Speed Record during a trip in January of 1988, and we also experienced the once in a lifetime Millennium Trip, ushering in a new century. For a guy who was born, raised and learned to fly in Wichita, Kansas, enjoying these adventures show how small aviation has made this world.

Clay, an icon in his military and civilian career, was close to retirement. He was a captain on the United Airlines 747SP, which is a long-range 747. He had dreamed of flying around the world in a commercial airliner, breaking the speed record. The record he was aiming to beat was 45 hours, 32 minutes, and 53 seconds. He also wanted to raise money for children's services in the Seattle area. He figured he would do both at the same time.

He asked United to help sponsor the trip by donating one of their planes. At first, they didn't want him to do it, but then thought it was a great idea after all of the positive publicity. Enthusiasm quickly grew and they were very pleased to be part of this historic adventure.

Although the plane could hold well over 200, Clay wanted fewer people to lighten the load, allowing for more fuel capacity. It's a long way around the world, and he wanted to do so with only two refueling stops. We had respect for one another and had given talks locally about aviation to clubs around town, and had socialized; so when I was invited, of course, I was excited.

The plane, a Boeing 747SP named the "Friendship One" took off from Seattle, Washington, on January 28, 1988, heading east with 141 people, exercise bicycles, a Volkswagen Jetta, fruit and regular bars, card games and foam mattresses. Most of us pilots stayed up in the cockpit, with six or seven in there most times. Flying around the world in a Boeing 747 and being with that many aviators, we had a lot of fun on the plane. Thirty-six hours, 54 minutes, and 15 seconds later, on January 30, 1988, we landed back in Seattle, breaking the world speed record by over eight hours!

It was an honor to fly with Clay Lacy as the captain, while setting a new around the world speed record. Among the passengers were astronaut and Apollo 11 Commander Neil Armstrong, Moya Lear, American businesswoman and wife of aviation pioneer Bill Lear, and Bob Hoover. There were over 100 standby passengers who wanted to go. The Jetta was auctioned off as the fastest VW in the world. We raised over $530,000 for children's charities in the Seattle area from that fun fundraising experience.

The Millennial Trip Predicted to Fail

I'm not sure if you were around back then, but it had been questioned if the world would end when the millennium changed to the year 2000 as much of technology was predicted to fail. By 1999, Clay owned his own 727 when he asked if Renae and I wanted to go with him to fly across the international dateline and be the first to arrive in the year 2000. And of course, we said yes. The flight was based in California, but we were scheduled to be in Hawaii. He flew to where we were, picked us up, and then went to Midway Island. Midway Island is midway across the Pacific Ocean, which is why it's called Midway. It was a very busy place during WWII because it was one of the few places a big airplane could land going to Asia. Until recently, if was also used for most of the major airlines flying in that direction because they required an alternative landing place for flying extended overwater trips.

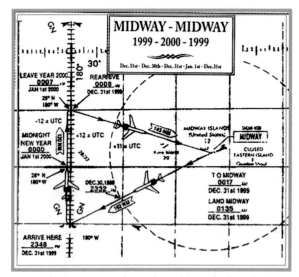

First flight in Y2K (2000) and last flight of 1999

Airplane technology has improved so that now they can make it without using Midway as an alternate airport.

The group of forty included Alex Kavassie, who worked for Bill Lear in Wichita (from the start of Lear) and was on both the Around the World Flight and the Millennium Flight. When we entered the year 2000, it was 4 am, December 31, 1999, on the West Coast. Within an hour, we traveled through five date changes before landing at Midway to celebrate the New Year. We were the first to cross the dateline and able to tell people everything was okay. Iridium Satellite had come out with a satellite telephone and could talk to anyone in the world. We called CNN to assure them there really was life on "the other side." Everybody had been talking about its effects and how all the electronic computers would fail to update creating chaos. So, we flew back and forth from 1999 to 2000. Clay Lacy repeatedly said during the flight, "Adios to 1999 and howdy to 2000."

All air carriers including ours had an FAA inspector in our dispatch room that night. I am not sure what they could have done if all the computers had quit, but like good government employees, they were there.

On the Lacy flight, all but one of our B-727 on-board computers reset back to 1999 each time, then clicked ahead to 2000. I never did find out that single computer's brand, nor did I ever decide if it was built better for not being flippy-floppy, or if it just had had enough of our running back and forth. We had at least five airline captains in the cockpit.

Clay Lacy has written a book titled *Lucky Me* and it is well worth reading.

132

Wichita, Kansas

Wichita is called the Air Capital of the World. Aviation and entrepreneurship have long thrived here.

Historical Foundation

I love Wichita because it truly is the Air Capital of the World. We have produced more airplanes in Wichita than have been produced anywhere else in the world. Especially if one is in the aviation business in any capacity, you can't find a better place to call home than Wichita. The pioneers helped establish this wonderful place. Bill Lear was born in 1902. Also a pilot, he pioneered the corporate jet, so there wasn't much competition back then. The first corporate jet was a Lear 23; built here in 1963, it held six passengers. I met Bill around 1965; he was a fun guy to know. At that time, we would go to Lear headquarters here in Wichita to do our aircraft maintenance at the factory, and he was still running the operations. Walter Beech died before I came to Wichita, but I knew his wife, Olive Ann Beech, and Lloyd Stearman, his cousin, who was also instrumental in envisioning the eventual construction of an Aviation Museum in Wichita. Clyde Cessna was also an aviator who lived in Wichita; we all knew each other.

A lot of people do not know the real story of how Wichita got its moniker. Three guys, Beech, Cessna and Stearman got together and convinced Jake Moellendick, an oil guy, to invest in their aircraft company, so they could build their first plane.

When that first aircraft took its first flight someone exclaimed, "There she goes! It looks just like a swallow."

And thus the plane and the factory got its first name, the Swallow Aircraft. Eventually, all three went their separate ways but remained friends. Cessna thought the wing should be on the top of the fuselage, Beech thought it should be on the bottom and Stearman put a wing on both the top and bottom. The start of Cessna, Beech and Stearman aircraft evolved. All three companies were extremely successful. Cessna and Beech are now owned by Textron and Stearman was bought out by Boeing during the Second World War. As a side note, one of the best designed planes was the Beech Staggerwing, with a wing on the top and bottom. It is still a great airplane. For the year that it was built, it was very modern, very comfortable, very fast, and good looking, too.

Kansas also has some of the wealthiest people per capita in the country primarily because we are such a strong oil and gas producing state, and we have lots of successful entrepreneurs. We are or were the home of the headquar-

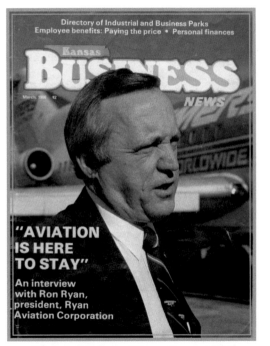

Directory of Industrial and Business Parks
Employee benefits: Paying the price • Personal finances

Kansas BUSINESS NEWS

March, 1986

"AVIATION IS HERE TO STAY"

An interview with Ron Ryan, president, Ryan Aviation Corporation

Kansas Business News Cover 1986

ters for Koch Industries, Via Christi, Pizza Hut, Coleman Camping, Rent-A-Center, Candlewood Suites, Value Place, Spirit Aerospace, Residence Inn and a lot of other great companies founded by true entrepreneurs.

Wichita has, and maintains, a great symphony orchestra and theatrical production companies. The downtown area is being revived quite successfully. Wichita has the Arkansas River, pronounced Ar-Kansas as in Kansas, flowing through the center of town. There are many parks and recreational areas which are clean and safe for our kids.

Community Service

It has been my pleasure to serve on many boards and committees, including the Kansas Water Commission, the Boy Scouts, the YMCA, Kansas Newman College, the Kansas Food Bank, Wichita's Downtown Development Committee, and the Kansas Advanced Technology Committee. I've also helped several nonprofits during my time in Wichita.

My wife Renae serves on the board of Friends University. Recently, we traveled with the Singing Quakers to Italy, Austria and a side trip to Bratislava and had a wonderful time on their concert tour. Both Renae and I served on the board of Kansas Newman University, a Catholic school years back.

> *Like my father-in-law Harvey always said and is engraved on his tombstone, "Do those things in life that will outlast you." Great advice. I pray I've done my best to do that.*

The Civilian and Military Communities

I was very active in our local Chamber of Commerce and took it upon myself, along with many others, to strengthen the ties between the Chamber/City/County and McConnell Air Force Base. I'm pleased our military feels both welcome and appreciated in Wichita. At one time, our Air National Guard unit was the largest in the nation and remains very active to this day. Presently, we house the KC-135 refueling tankers and will have the new Boeing refuelers, KC-46s, stationed at McConnell.

We have a lot of airmen and women who retire from the Air Force and stay in Wichita, thereby contributing greatly to our community's success. Recently, I was asked by the commander of McConnell if I would be an Honorary Colonel. I proudly and gladly accepted. It is heartwarming, and gives me optimism about our country's future to see these young airmen and women serving in such a professional way defending our way of life and liberty.

The Tuskegee Airmen

Several years back, I chaired the Kansas Aviation Task Force, serving with some members who flew the red-tailed P-51 Mustangs of the Tuskegee Airmen. The Tuskegee Airmen were a group of African American pilots during WW II that were assigned P-51 Mustangs to fly to protect our bombers. At first, the "white" pilots gave them a hard time, but they soon found out the "black" pilots were not only doing their jobs, but doing them in a spectacular way. They saved many, many white guys' asses. Assembling and training that elite group of airmen has gone down in history as one of the best decisions our military ever made. There are several books and movies about these brave aviation fighters.

Closed minds need to open. Even as a kid, I loved traveling. One of my first out of town trips was with my girlfriend's parents. They had family in Valdosta, Georgia, and were taking a trip around Thanksgiving to visit. They asked if I wanted to go with them and immediately, I said, "Yes!" The car trip was uneventful, but when we got into the home of their relatives, it was an eye opener for me.

Their relatives were middle class and had a very modest home. They had a black nanny who helped cook, wash clothes and take care of the kids. She was as much a part of their family as anyone in my mind. When she stepped out of the door, it was as if she was an alien. For a young person like me, it was shocking. Even I could tell how wrong that was.

When we would go downtown, the African Americans would make sure they did not walk on the same side of the street any of us white folks were on. This was my first up-close encounter with segregation. I couldn't believe it. They could come into your home and do your work and help raise your kids, but still were considered less than second class citizens. I shudder today to think of the injustices so many Blacks suffered. Like the black pilot or soldier, women were discriminated against and not recognized for their talents and service. It's sad and very unfair. We have come a long way baby, but still have a ways to go.

The Midian Shriners Fez

Having said that, that was yesterday and hopefully we won't need many more generations before we realize we are all God's children regardless of color or gender. These experiences left a lifetime impression on me. God created all of us equal. It is what we choose to do with the few days we have here on earth that matters.

The bottom line is, it all comes down to people and how they interact with each other. Wichita is a very giving community. Fundraisers are frequent and are almost always successful. People caring about people happens here, and should happen everywhere. I've said it before: when we meet our Maker, the color of our skin will be irrelevant; but how we treated each other will be what matters. I know our Lord and Savior Jesus Christ had to have had dark colored skin. Aren't some people going to be surprised!

The Flying Fezzes

I did become a Mason with the intention to eventually become a Shriner. One must be a Mason before joining the Shriners. In our Shriner unit, we formed the Flying Fezzes where we would fly burned or immobilized kids either to Brownsville, Texas, or St. Louis, Missouri, for treatment at no cost. The Shriner hospitals do fantastic work helping kids and do it for free.

Some of the cases would make you cry when you see the pain and suffering those kids were experiencing, especially the burn victims. We often flew the same kids more than once, as burn patients need to go get their skin cut frequently to allow for growth because burned skin will not allow for expansion.

Another unfortunately frequent trip was to San Diego with cancer patients who wanted to get care in Mexico with treatments not approved in the US. Sometimes it worked and other times, not so good. Yet, we did what we could. Thank heavens we now have a "right to try." It's a new law that allows experimental drugs on patients that have been deemed to be terminal.

He who is given much, owes much. Even if you don't have a plane, we have been so blessed in this country, so for us not to give back some of what we've been given is a sin. It all belongs to God anyway. I've also found it to be true that the more you give the more you receive, as long as you're not giving to get. Tithing is essential. Unfortunately, the government asks for more than even God does. Shriner Hospitals are miracle workers and it was our privilege to serve them.

Wagonmasters

The goal of the Wagonmasters is to enjoy the good life in Wichita and raise money to give to charitable organizations. I've been part of the organization for over 32 years.

Another great honor in my life was when I was selected to be the 41st Admiral Windwagon Smith of the Wichita River Festival for the year 2014. This was and is a great civic honor since the Admiral is the mascot for the nine-day outdoor Wichita River Festival.

Wichita's River Festival is no small deal. It is a nine-day outdoor affair where one buys a $10 button for adults and $5 for kids that gets you into all the events, including those with popular entertainers. We have great corporate sponsorship and about 9,000 volunteers that make the 44 year running event such a great family success. Mary Beth Jarvis has been the CEO of the event for the last several years (recently retired) and has done a yeoman's or yeowoman's job. They also put on an "Autumn in Art" festival in the fall which draws participants and spectators from all over the world.

One year, Wichita put on an aviation festival at Jabara Airport, and I was selected to be the honorary host of the two day event. The best part of this experience was getting to meet and know a little better some of the top aviation performers in the world including Patty Wagstaff. Did I mention Wichita is a great place to live?

Renae Ryan and Ron Ryan
as Windwagon Smith XLI

The Clapp House

L.W. Clapp was a Wichita Mayor from 1917-1919 and a Wichita City Manager from 1919-1921. The City of Wichita owned his three-story Victorian home sitting on three acres of land close to downtown Wichita. The house had been vacant for about five years and was in terrible shape. Broken windows, bird droppings and vacant home wear and tear had taken its toll. What it did have was lots of hand carved woodwork, staircases and doors along with lincrusta walls, parquet floors and potential charm. Jack McInteer had taken me to see the house and said he wanted to buy it, fix it up and set up his legal offices there. His wife Sandi told him to just go ahead and get the divorce papers if he did this, and leave her out of it. Well, the city put the house up for sale via a sealed bid. I bid on the house and oops, I got it!

I had two architectural firms give me bids on fixing up the place. I doubled their estimates in my mind before bidding. While fixing up the home that was built in 1886, we decided to make sure the construction would last at least another 100 years. After the fix up, I should have quadrupled their estimate. We did make it a Decorator's Showhouse; which served as a fund raiser for the Wichita Symphony. We didn't move in until the show was over. The house was on the National Historic Register. They were a real pain to deal with but, the final product was fantastic. After living there for several years, we eventually donated the home back to the city.

The Kansas Aviation Museum

Spending most of my aviation career in Wichita has been great. I have had the chance to know Bill Lear, Moya Lear, Olive Ann Beech, Dwayne Wallace, Russ Meyer, several commanders at McConnell AFB, Charlie Johnson, Clay Lacy, Bob Hoover, Alex Kavassie, Al Higdon, Jeff Turner, Tom Gentiles, Brian Barents, Clyde Stearman, Lyndon Blue, Harry Combs and the list of aviation's greatest goes on and on.

I have worked for over 30 years with the Kansas Aviation Museum (KAM). The museum was started by a group of caring citizens, the Wichita Aeronautical Historic Association, (WAHA). The purpose of the museum is to retain and teach the story and history of aviation in Wichita and Kansas. I still serve on the KAM's board.

We now have the old municipal terminal building located at McConnell AFB. The building itself is on the Nation Historic Register and is owned by the City of Wichita, although supported by private donations. Between the city owning the building and the NHR controlling any improvements, it is a constant challenge to keep the building in proper shape, but we somehow have continued to make it happen.

The building has hosted some famous folks including Fred Astaire, who danced in the lobby, Amelia Earhart came through, and Charles Lindbergh visited several times. Many other celebrities and politicians like Orville Wright, Ginger Rogers, Will Rodgers and Wiley Post spent time in this beautiful building. Wichita was a convenient halfway fuel stop for a lot of cross-country flyers.

Securing the Building

We were able to secure the building after I got a call from Colonel Ed Sykes, former Commander of the Air National Guard, asking if I wanted the old terminal building for our air museum. I said yes, and he said we had better act fast as the Guard was scheduled to tear the building down and build a new guard headquarters. Ed, plus the current Base Commander, who also was in favor of saving the building, and I flew to DC to meet at the Pentagon with the General in charge.

At first, he said no way did he want an air museum located next to the Air Base. At that time, the B-1B had been assigned to McConnell and the Air Force was having some bad press over some operational problems. I told the

Wichita Municipal Airport aerial view

General what a great way to promote the B-1B from the tower and flight ramp at the proposed museum site. The public could see the planes flying and feel better about the huge investment made developing them. He agreed, and after a lot of paperwork, the building was "given" to the City of Wichita and leased to KAM.

Like most non-profit organizations, the Kansas Aviation Museum constantly struggles to have enough money to not just keep its doors open, but to continue to improve the displays and historic records and maintain the many historic aircraft we have on display. One of our goals is when someone has seen the displays and artifacts, they will want to come back and bring their friends. KAM does a lot of STEM (Science, Technology, Engineering and Math) activities. Lots of kids visit and love what they see.

Why the aviation manufacturers in Wichita haven't stepped up and given KAM much better support still escapes me to this day. However, that seems to be slowly changing. We have gotten some support from the city and county, but if we are to retain the title of Air Capital of the World, this site can go a long way in making that happen. McConnell AFB with the Guard brings a large amount of money into our community, and thankfully, the base and the community have always had an excellent relationship. One of the best benefits McConnell offers is the amount of talented people who retire from the base and remain and serve in our community.

KAM also houses the Kansas Aviation Hall of Fame and the Kansas Governor's Aviation Awards. The gallery is loaded with some of the greatest pioneers and entrepreneurs in aviation history.

The museum desperately needs a display hangar to protect some of the general aviation planes we now must keep outside in the weather. We have about 30 other vintage aircraft stored in a 'barn' that need to be reassembled, but can't until we have a place inside to store and show them. I think we have an obligation to preserve and show off our rich aviation heritage and those pioneers who often gave their lives to bring aviation to life.

More Planes, More Opportunities

At the Kansas Aviation Museum we have restored several vintage aircraft and have numerous Kansas-built airplanes both large and small on our ramp. We have many more in pieces and parts needing restoration, but we desperately need a hangar to protect these priceless planes from the elements. So, if you have a few extra bucks, the museum would sure appreciate any help they can get. KAM is a 501(c) (3). Like most museums, they are always long on ideas, but short on money. The many inside displays over and above the airplanes are also informative, interesting, and historic and well worth your time visiting. In addition to the regular active duty airmen, there is a large Air National Guard unit at McConnell, and both the Air Force as well as the Guard, have been helpful with some of KAM's needs. We are, and will remain, the Air Capital of the World, and proud of it.

When I used to fly about everywhere in the world with the airline, I was often asked where I was from. When I said, "Wichita, Kansas," I would get a blank stare until I asked them to just look out on their aircraft ramp and count the planes built in Wichita. Then I would say Boeing, Beech, Cessna and Lear were also from there. It got their attention.

Among so many aircraft from Wichita's past, we have a V-tail Beechcraft Bonanza, a massive Boeing B-52, along with a Boeing 727 and a Boeing 737 that I donated to the museum some years back, both of which figure in some of the stories related in these pages. We have an original Learjet, a Cessna Citation, several military Wichita built aircraft plus many vintage aircraft like the two Stearmans on display. Volunteers are putting finishing touches on our rebuilt Beech Staggerwing. Make sure you visit the Kansas Aviation Museum to view these beautiful planes. To learn more about Kansas Aviation, I recommend "Prairie Runways" by Susan Thompson and "Wichita: Where Aviation Took Wing" by The Greteman Group.

Restoring Doc

A few years back, I was asked if I would be willing to serve on the board of a new entity called "Doc's Friends." "Doc" is a glistening, thundering, imposing fully-restored World War II B-29 bomber that lay inert and alone out in the chalky China Lake Naval Air Station in the California desert. Tony Mazzolini, of Ohio, was the inspiration and dreamer who brought Doc out of the desert and eventually to Wichita. At the time, there was only one B-29 flying and that belonged to, and was operated by, the Confederate Air Force now called the Commemorative Air Force.

Fifteen years ago, we gently, respectfully approached the lonesome old warrior, brought it to Wichita in seven semi-trucks in pieces, and slowly and methodically, put it back into flying condition.

Tony was able to talk to Jeff Turner, the former head of Boeing Wichita and later Spirit Aerospace, and Jeff agreed to help. Jeff told Tony if he got the plane to Wichita, he would put it together. Jeff has been the driving force behind this project.

Tony spent years and more money than he even had to save Doc. Boeing, Spirit Aerospace and over 500,000 volunteer hours went into the restoration of Doc. In fact, one volunteer is now 92 years old and is an original Rosie the Riveter. Connie actually put rivets in this very airplane when it was built in Wichita, and now has worked again on the same plane. A lot of the original rivets were still good. She is a delight and a passing part of our great history. It was pure joy to see the wonder in her eyes as she was

Restored WWII B-29 "Doc"
(Photo Courtesy of Paul Bowen)

helped up into Doc and taken up and around our city in what is now only the second flying B-29 in the world---the bomber she'd helped to build - twice!

I can tell you it is in a lot better shape than the day it first came out of the factory. When they built these great planes, they knew they may only fly one or two missions before being shot down or destroyed. The reconstruction was carried out by retired Boeing employees who knew what they were doing and did it right. We recently built Doc a hangar with a learning center. What a beauty and magnificent historical flying museum they make. If you are ever close to Wichita, come to the Dwight D. Eisenhower airport and tour this wonder that was originally built in Wichita in 1944.

Many American airmen gave their lives defending this great country while flying these monuments to their deaths. And it was the sight, sounds, and payloads of these B-29s that finally convinced the world's tyrants and bullies, America was done with the war.

I am proud that I got asked to serve along with several other board members on this project. My hope is that generations yet to come will have the opportunity to enjoy and learn from this venture. A great big thanks to Tony and Jeff for making this happen.

I strongly encourage all who appreciate flying, freedom's history, and Wichita's heritage, to financially support Doc's Friends, and the ongoing work of the Kansas Aviation Museum.

Did I tell you I think Wichita is a great place to live?

Faith, Family and Friends

Without God, everything is impossible. With God, everything is possible.

You have to have a fundamental moral foundation to work from, and having faith in God gives us that moral foundation. I have gotten some of my best ideas in my sleep, through my dreams. I feel it was God giving me information and inspiration, talking to me, guiding me and directing me to take certain key steps in my business and personal life. I would literally wake up some mornings with answers having envisioned what to do in my dreams. And still do.

I learned to write down whatever came to me in the middle of the night. When I didn't write some of those things down, I would forget by morning. I guess what I'm saying is, if you listen, you'll hear what you need to know.

My Three Sons

I have three boys: Dale, Mark and Scott, and now I have six grandkids and seven great-grandkids. I tell my boys jokingly that having grandkids is a lot more fun than having kids.

My oldest son Dale has patented an electric quadracycle for the handicapped where you can ride your wheelchair on a platform and drive the electric quadracycle with your hands. He and his wife Kara have a new venture growing microgreens in

Dale Ryan

Mark and Scott Ryan

Kingman, Kansas. Dale's eldest daughter Alicia, and husband Corey, have three kids; Walker, Grayson, and Anson who are a total delight to Renae and me. Dale's youngest daughter, Jessica, just graduated from KU Medical Center, so we now have a doctor in the house. Jessica's son Kayden lives in Houston.

My middle son Mark is on the move still trying to find himself and figure out life. Unfortunately, he has had lots of hard bumps on that road. He is driving for Uber and is just getting by, but remains in my hopes and prayers. That being said, some things you do out of love, and choosing to raise his child Lexi changed our lives completely.

One day while at our lake home in Oklahoma, we received a call saying the State had our 10-year-old granddaughter, Lexi, in Hiawatha, Kansas, and if we could get there by five o'clock that evening, we could have her. Otherwise, she would be put into Kansas State custody the next day, and it would be very difficult to get her out. The plane was in the shop, so we drove to Hiawatha and picked up this ragamuffin of a girl.

Her dad is my middle son who had been using drugs since he was in high school. Her mother had severe bipolar issues and was pregnant at sixteen with Lexi's older brother. Their family life was a disaster.

They fought in front of the children and broke up many times. We decided if we were going to try to raise her, we didn't want to do it in North Miami Beach. We sold our Aventura condo, boat and boat slip, and took her to our home at Grand Lake. After one school year in that area, we chose to buy a house in Wichita, and moved her into a Christian school there. Through it all, Lexi did well in school and is now doing quite well in life. She is enrolled at Wichita State University taking psychology courses, has her own apartment and a full-time job at a private school. Her brother Xavier is married and employed, lives in Kansas City, and has two cute kids born in the same year, Ellie and William. We keep praying for their well-being and happiness.

From Left: Ron, Xavier, Renae and Lexi

My youngest son Scott was a co-owner of 11 Meineke Car Care Centers located throughout Wichita and Hutchinson, Kansas, and Tulsa, Oklahoma. We recently sold the franchise. He moved to live his dream, with his wife Rhonda, to the Lake of the Ozarks. He's one of the best mechanics I know. Amanda and Kayla are Scott's two girls. Amanda and her husband Levi are wonderful parents and have three cute children Lathan, Callan and baby girl Rowen. Kayla Bell is single, and a sweetheart.

Fatherhood

If I have any regrets in my life, it is not spending enough meaningful time with my boys while they were young. I thought building a business and working to see that they could have a secure financial future was the way to go. It wasn't and isn't.

I still see too many fathers place their time in the wrong things, as nothing should be more important than one's family. Yes, building a business demands a lot of time, but make sure the way you spend your time is worth it. We have a limited amount of time, and that is why flying, a time saver, is such an important part of living.

Ryan Fun & Fitness

Trust the Government???

My youngest brother Bob loves sports and once was a top ranked racquetball player. A group of doctors in West Burlington, Iowa, had built a health club, but due to the changing tax laws, they wanted to get rid of it. Bob found out about it and told me. I talked to the doctors and was able to negotiate a price agreeable to all of us.

My oldest son Dale was looking for something to do, so I was able to convince him to move from Kansas City to Burlington to run the club. One of the first things he wanted to do was remodel it, add a bar and make it a 24-hour operation. He worked at it a couple of years and found he just couldn't compete with the YMCA. We talked about what to do and decided we would try to sell it or, better yet, wait until after the first of the year and donate it to the Y.

We officially closed it the first week in December 1989, but my mother, aunt and other friends could go there and work out at their leisure. I'd decided on the latter of the two choices, to donate it to the Y if they would take it. My new USPS contract was starting in January. So, my income would go up substantially the next year when a tax deduction would be more meaningful.

I had married Renae in November of 1989, and received a call from my son Dale on December 31st that the club was on fire!

Things went downhill from there. He called back a little later and said two firemen were missing. I immediately dressed and got our Learjet out. As soon as my attorney,

Jack McInteer, could get there, we flew to Burlington. When we flew over the site, the building was still burning.

Investigators had found that the two firemen, for whatever reason, had left their hose and got lost and trapped in a corner and died. We found out later, that at the time those two firefighters entered the building, it was only filled with thick smoke. However, others were breaking in the back door. That sudden opening created a backdraft allowing oxygen to ignite in the super-heated smoke causing the firefighters to panic.

The fire marshal for the State of Iowa investigated the fire and would not let any of our insurance or investigators on the premises. Using an end loader, they scooped up what remained of the entire interior and dumped it in the outside parking lot. We waited for several days to find out what the ruling was as to the cause. They said they were ruling it arson as the racquetball courts had classic accelerant burn patterns on the hardwood floors.

We hired a lawyer to represent Dale and privately retained another local lawyer for two reasons: We never believed it was arson; but if it was, Dale had nothing to do with it. In retrospect, hiring the local attorney was a mistake. After 18 months, the federal government charged my son with arson.

Until this time, I never seriously thought we had dishonest federal prosecutors.

I was wrong.

A woman named Linda Reade was the prosecutor who lied, fabricated her own facts and distorted the truth to get a conviction on my son. He was sentenced to 27 years in prison.

I was devastated and hired top notch attorneys from Washington D.C.. Finally, after 10 years of my son being in prison, and two appearances before the United States Supreme Court, the case was finally seen to be bogus, thrown out, and my son released.

The new investigators found the burn patterns on the floor could just as easily have come from melted wax, light ballasts, and other ceiling material falling. We also found the prosecution had taken some of the intact floor-

ing, so they knew it wouldn't burn and knew something else could have caused the patterns. But, they withheld that knowledge, just as they had with other exculpatory evidence. Pouring accelerants on the floor and igniting it, would not create a burn pattern like they were claiming, and they knew this, but hid the information.

Ms. Reade was an ambitious prosecutor who wanted to become a judge, a promotion she later received. In later years (2010-2013), Judge Reade was caught in another questionable prosecution. It was also reversed, and the defendant/prisoner released.

Those intent on assuring Dale was convicted even went so far as to erect a statue in front of the West Burlington fire department in honor of the fallen two, and put on the statue it was Dale who killed them. They had to remove that sign when the USSC freed Dale. The parents of the two men were very nasty to us, but one of their wives talked to us in private, and was very kind – a small light for which we were grateful.

This may shock you, but the federal government can be corrupt. They had my phones wiretapped and lied about it in court. They had done fire testing and kept that from the court because it didn't comply with their theories. On several occasions, the prosecution had offered my son a reduced sentence if he'd say I told him to burn down the building. I guess Ms. Reade thought I would be a bigger fish to hook, resulting in even more publicity for her. This was the top news story in Iowa for two years.

After Dale's conviction, I made Jeff Crippen president of our airline, so I could spend time proving my son's innocence. Jeff did an outstanding job, and was with us up until we sold the second time. He had Ms. Beth Paladino, our controller, working by his side. She worked hard and smart and contributed greatly to our success. Renae and I will forever be grateful to the teams we had in place. I can't say enough good things of Ray Thomas, John Wilson, David Ray, Art Seabolt, Mary McGoldrich, Jack McInteer, Derry Larson, Betty Crumrine, and Bill Green.

Early Influences

One thing is for certain: God knew what influences I'd need from an early age and He provided them. I don't mean to backtrack, but the longer I live, the more important I believe it is to understand the forces that shape our lives.

My mom would make all of us kids go to church every Sunday, which sometimes was a real chore. She came from a farm family of nine kids. My grandmother had lost two of her kids in their youth; one at birth and another less than two years old. My mother had five brothers and two sisters who lived. In those days, the death of a youngster was unfortunately very common. I can't say I ever got used to it, but Mom and my grandma helped by not shielding me from it, either. Their combined influences informed my outlook on life and death.

My mother was extremely smart and married my dad at the age of

Ron Ryan's Mother Mildred Ryan

16. She always had straight As in school and could work the newspaper jumbles and cross word puzzles in a flash. There is a game called Balderdash where you need to guess fabricated words from a true one, and she was no fun to play with because she could answer the unique questions correctly. Though unable to continue in school, Mom was brilliant and never stopped her education. I never heard her whine about any of her life experiences. She made a lot of lemonade out of what life tossed in front of her, and could've been or done anything to which she set her mind.

In my youth, World War II was raging. All five of my maternal uncles enlisted in the Navy. One served on a submarine, one was on a destroyer, another on a battleship and one was a Seabee, the Navy's construction battalion.

I'm not sure in what part of the Navy my fifth uncle served. I do know I loved it when they came home on leave wearing their Navy uniforms and sailor caps.

The one who became a Seabee, Uncle Willy, would go into areas that were going to be invaded and do demolition to assist in the invasion, a very dangerous duty. He was scheduled to go on one mission when he came down with appendicitis. His team went out on a demolition assignment while he was in the hospital, and to this day no one knows what happened. The entire team was lost.

Willy always suffered with survivor's guilt about losing his friends while he was hospitalized. Although he was not an alcoholic, he did drink a lot to try to forget this tragedy and grieved over other missions where good men were lost. Fortunately, none of my uncles lost their lives in the war, but they would rarely talk about their experiences. It was too painful because they'd witnessed death up close and personal.

Ruby, my mother's older sister and best friend, helped raise us kids when mother was working. And years later when my Agriboard plant burned down in Texas, she was the first one to say, "How can I help?" Ruby was a role model for me, a beautiful woman who never had any children of her own and treated us as hers. I think that is why she was so good to our family.

Ruby lived with us during the war while her husband, Bill, served in the Army. Remember what I said about God knowing what influences I'd need? This wasn't by chance. Bill built very nice large, wooden boats for a living. They eventually moved to Florida, where my Dad really wanted to go, but my mom would not leave her kids in Iowa to go to Florida.

Bill knew he was an alcoholic, so he rarely drank. It always amazed me that some of his so-called friends would coax him into taking a drink, knowing if he took one, he couldn't stop until he passed out. Who needs friends like that?

After his death, Ruby was working at a boat yard in Florida when a single guy by the name of Perry Stevens came in to get his boat serviced. When they met, it was love at first sight.

They traveled the US by boat, motor home and car. Perry would often tell me there isn't enough time in life to just visit all the great places in the US, let alone the world. Perry said he'd live to 100, but he lived to 102. Although they were quite wealthy, they never let their wealth go to their head. Perry and his sister were raised on a sandy, hardscrabble,

Great-Grandparents using steamboat travel on Mississippi

dirt-poor Texas ranch, where he grew up riding on cattle drives to make a living. He was a true cowboy. One day they found this black, oozy stuff called oil on the ranch, and suddenly, he and his sister became very wealthy.

Neither Ruby nor Perry had any kids, but they were great philanthropists. They set up a charitable organization for children's homes which still exists today. Perry never forgot his roots. He and Ruby supported many other worthy charities, too. Ruby died a couple of years ago, but up until her death, she was giving money to causes she believed in. I am glad I had enough generous people in my life that I learned being generous feels really good and is the right thing to do. Being blessed enough to be a blessing describes my family. We don't get to pick our family, but I have been blessed beyond all measure with my family.

Our family was always very close, though we were spread apart over many years. I think our relationships all centered around our belief in Christ and the church. My oldest brother Wayne and younger brother Larry chose being a pastor as a way of life. They were both full-time pastors. I never even considered it. They just needed somebody to pray for, a lot, so I gladly filled that spot.

My oldest brother, Wayne, became a Christian in his early teens and wound up marrying his lifelong girlfriend, Elda. Wayne went to Asbury College for six years and, when he graduated, he took a job at a small Iowa church preaching for $40.00 a week. I thought, "Wow! After six years, $40.00 a week?" Even in those early years, God was impressing on me His economy doesn't work anything like that of the world; and that He pays in ways beyond finding out. A few years back, Elda died. When any of us would suggest to Wayne to try dating, he would get mad at us for even making that suggestion. With Wayne being a preacher all of his life, he met a lot of people. One of those women was Trish from his home church who he fortunately fell in love with and married. She has been, and continues to be, a super asset and loved member of our family. She is a joy to be around.

My younger brother Larry was dating a girl in Burlington, and they both became believers. It wasn't fair, I tell you. I was surrounded! I asked Wayne once how it was he didn't go to movies and all the other things that I saw as unfair restrictions. I still retained the notion being a Christian consisted of giving up everything fun and enjoyable. His answer was simple. "I just don't care to."

In the summer, I went to church camp in Fairfield, Iowa, about 40 miles from Burlington. I went forward and accepted Christ as my Savior. Like the old song says, "What a difference since Jesus passed by." My life did a 180. Christ made all the difference, and still does! I now understand what my brothers were saying.

I haven't always been a model Christian, sometimes far from it, though I know we all should strive to be at our best for God. I do know though, that the really important thing for salvation is to believe in Christ as our Savior. As the saying goes, sitting in church doesn't make you a Christian any more than standing in your hangar makes you a Cessna. Believing in Jesus Christ as Savior is what makes the difference. If you do that, whether you plan it or not, your life changes for the better.

Clockwise from Left: Glenn, Larry, Gayla, Renae, Marilyn, Ron, Charlene, David, Elda and Wayne

My brothers and I spent a lot of time on the river. I learned to water ski early. Living in Iowa, it got cold early in the year and stayed cold late. We would run our boats until we could no longer break through the ice, then put them back in the river in the spring, while the melting ice was still flowing.

One day, while there was still ice in the river, my uncle Fritz and his wife Red went water skiing. We had wet suits, but if you went into the water, it was still very cold. I had my uncle behind the boat when we ran out of gas, and it looked like he was going to crawl up the ski rope, so we changed tanks and went on. When we got to the dock, I went out and he drove. He tried to dump me, but failed, and I skied back in and sat on the dock, never once going into the water.

Like a kid, after he parked and tied up the boat, I was teasing him for getting wet. While I was taking off my wet suit, he pushed me in. My own uncle! I still remember the cold shock, and it was a good thing I was young, for I've no idea what the sudden shock might have done if I was older. It suddenly dawned on me that Uncle Fritz had been in unfriendly, cold water during the war years when in the Navy. I never forgot that lesson. Things may not seem dangerous on the surface, but hazards lurk for the unwary. Fritz and Red played an important role in my young days. I was privileged to have them in my life.

My siblings are, in order from oldest to youngest, Wayne, Charlene, me, Barbara, Marilyn, Larry and Bobby.

I've talked about Wayne and Trish, and Larry and Gayla. Charlene, whose deceased husband David was like a brother, is my older sister who everyone thought was my twin. She's the one who had polio.

Sister Marilyn, a dedicated Christian, lived on a farm with her husband Glenn until he recently died. She's one of God's unique creatures. Barbara is the one who died too young. Bobby is married to Paula. He is the youngest and the most athletic and energetic of all of us.

Relatives can be important. They are family. A lot of

145

people set money as their goal and that is a terrible mistake. You should make money accomplishing your goal, rather than setting money as your goal. My family helped shape my life in a positive way, and I was blessed because that's not always true of all families. Success is what you make of it. Success is different things to different people.

Friendship and Love

As you now know, I have traveled a lot all over the world mostly in my job. When I sold the company the second time, I told my good friends Jack, my lawyer, and Derry Larson, my accountant, that Renae and I want to travel as tourists and see as much of the world as we can.

Best friends, best times, best travels. What can we say? We can talk about the times we were climbing the Sydney Bridge in Australia, New Zealand Milford Sound, the steps at Machu Picchu, the Three Gorges Dam in China, Kentucky Derby, sightseeing flights over Mount Everest, Ireland and the Winding Stairs Café, the Amazon River, visiting with children in India, and of course, Israel. Some of our journeys included riding camels, elephants, horses or mules down the Grand Canyon; not to mention the planes and cruise ships. Derry and I playing thousands of hands of gin rummy. Kay, his wife, tries to keep Derry in line, and is the first one to always sign up on a trip, willing to try most things.

Jack remains the forever best travel planner/guide, and his wife Sandi is the best dizzy and caring girl I know.

Travel Buddies from left: Renae, Jack, Ron, Sandi, Kay and Derry

Though she suffers from vertigo due to Meniere's disease, she's still adventurous and makes the best travel memory books ever.

There is a lot more world to see than there is time to see it. We have several more trips scheduled…

Renae and I also met what turned out to be very good friends, Joan and Garry Deuel. We met them on a cruise. Their name tags were misspelled, showing Joabie and Farie. That remained their names with us. We did several cruises together as well as spend time at different resorts just having good clean fun. We were together in Mexico for a week and Garry developed a cough. When he returned home, they found he had lung cancer and gave him no more than six months to live. When we heard this, Renae and I went to California to visit and say goodbye. We had a great time together, but shortly after, Garry went to be with his Maker. As one gets older, one experiences a lot more deaths and sickness in the world. Joan is a super trooper and is weathering the storm well.

The good news is Joan has recently found what appears to be a great guy. We have been trying to get to California to meet him but this virus thing has kept us at home. Joan was concerned that my close friendship with Garry might be a problem for me. Before Garry died, we had talked about this issue, and he wanted me to help her find someone worthy of her love. That is the same wish I have for my wife Renae should something happen to me.

Enjoy your friendships while you have them.

Israel - the Heartbeat of the World

You don't have to be big to be important.

Renae and I have been to Israel at least eight times. Pastor Gene Williams led us on our first trip. We would usually go with a group of pastors, but have gone on family trips as well. What an incredibly small piece of geography to be so important and contain so much history that has shaped, and is continuing to shape, the world!

I've been to most places in the world at least once, and I admit I really wasn't all that excited about going to Israel the first time. But once there, it was the most impressive place in the world I have ever been. A local TV station was filming for an Easter series and had five different preachers of different denominations accompany them. Talk about interesting commentary! I loved it, and after the first trip, we made plans to return.

Ron getting baptized in the Jordan River

I will never forget the first day in the van pulling up in front of the Gaza Gate with the armed guards above the gate, and the money changers at the gate along with camels and sheep. I thought about what it must have looked like when Jesus walked on some of those same streets. I'm sure the steps going up to where the old Temple had stood are the same steps that once felt the rasp of Jesus' own sandals. It was a heart-changing experience, standing where we knew our Savior once stood.

On one of our trips, we had just left a tourist spot overlooking the Sea of Galilee. We had stopped a couple of miles down the road and were looking at some other sights when we heard gunfire. All the drivers had radios, and they herded us quickly back to the vehicles. They made us get in and leave because the Palestinians had just shot and killed several young Israeli girls who were on a tour, right where we were just a few minutes earlier. That's indicative of what man is thoughtlessly doing on Holy Ground.

Words can't describe the places of history; the Garden Tomb, Golgotha, Masada, the Dead Sea and the stark, barren caves where the Dead Sea Scrolls were found. Each place has such significance; and to be able to visit and meditate in those spaces, is almost overwhelming. I was privileged to have Gene Williams baptize me in the Jordan River. Even after eight trips, I feel there is still so much to see and experience, I plan on going back. If those scenes don't give you "goose bumps," then I doubt anything will.

Life's a one-day-at-a-time opportunity to have a good or bad day. If you make more of them good, then you will have a good life. So far, it has worked for me, and I continue to pray for my children as well as the rest of my family. It took me a lot of years, and a lot of heartache, to learn just how important family is.

I've read that "you will be the same person in five years as you are today, except for the people you meet and the books you read." I believe that. Show me who you hang with, what you spend your time watching and reading, and I'll show you what you are, and who you're becoming. If you look at a person's checkbook, you can tell a lot about what kind of person they are; giving, caring, selfish or self-centered.

There are two types of people here on earth; one is grateful and the other ungrateful. That choice makes an incredible difference in how one views their life. Happy or miserable; life is a choice.

To Wrap it Up

They say, "With every adversity there is opportunity." That certainly has been true during my entire life. Not getting hired by TWA seemed a terrible disappointment, but thank God I did not get hired. The fiasco with Eastern Airlines was also heart wrenching, but again the good Lord was watching over me. Having the gear stick on the Cessna 310 allowed me to fly in the Lear and get a job in Wichita flying for Jack DeBoer. When Jack had financial problems in the early 70's, that allowed me to start DeBoer Aviation with Jack's wife as my partner. Jack's continuing financial woes allowed George Ablah to be my partner in the aviation business, where we grew it and sold it for a nice profit. That allowed me to buy it back two years and one day later, where I owned all the stock and air carrier certificate.

When George had financial trouble, I was able to help him finance several large real estate deals where we both made a good profit. When George had worked his way back financially and didn't need my help anymore, he continued to include me in his real estate deals up until his death. These are but a few of the adversities I encountered, and in almost every case, positive results ensued.

Cheers to my wife and life!

We have no mountains or oceans here in Wichita but we have some of the best people in the world and have found this a great place to raise a family. Having lived eighty-two years, I have a lot more memories and stories, but I tried to remember ones that might be of interest.

If I had my life to live over, the biggest change I would make is spending more quality time with my family. My three sons are grown and their kids have kids. I tell them I only wish I could have started with my grandkids. Now that they have children and grands, they understand.

None of us gets to choose our parents or family members, but if I had been able to do so, I would not change a thing. Being blessed with great loving parents and siblings can't be measured, as it is priceless and shapes who we are. Taking our families for granted is a sad thing for all involved. Way too many realize this after it is too late to correct. I still strongly believe in the Proverbs 23:7: "As a man thinketh in his heart, so is he." That is so very true. We are a collection of our thoughts and choices.

Although I have had a heart attack, two stents plus prostate cancer and now a new valve in my heart, I am still in very good health. I'm between flight medicals, but plan on getting that back again soon. When I had my heart attack over ten years ago, I thought there was a good likelihood I might die, but I found although I didn't want to die, I was ready to meet God.

What a comforting feeling to know there is something more than just this life here on earth, and that "something more" is actually Someone more, and of far greater importance than what we have here. The old saying is so true, "We ain't going to get out of this world alive." All of us need to just make sure we KNOW where we will be spending our eternity.

I hope you enjoyed sharing a small piece of my history.

Safe flying.

Traveling in airplanes is the best way man can buy more time. You can get more things done if you don't spend so much time traveling. If you knew you were going to die tomorrow, how much would you pay for a little extra time?